S0-AKX-370

LIFE LESSONS
from the
HIDING PLACE

Discovering the Heart of
CORRIE TEN BOOM

PAM ROSEWELL MOORE

Chosen
Grand Rapids, Michigan

© 2004 by Pam Rosewell Moore

Published by Chosen Books
a division of Baker Publishing Group
P.O. Box 6287, Grand Rapids, MI 49516-6287
www.chosenbooks.com

Printed in the United States of America

All rights reserved. No part of this publication may be reproduced, stored in a retrieval system, or transmitted in any form or by any means—for example, electronic, mechanical, photocopy, recording—without the prior written permission of the publisher. The only exception is brief quotations in printed reviews.

Library of Congress Cataloging-in-Publication Data
Moore, Pamela Rosewell.
    Life lessons from the hiding place: discovering the heart of Corrie ten Boom
/ Pam Rosewell Moore.
       p.   cm.
    Includes bibliographical references and index.
    ISBN 0-8007-9354-4 (pbk.)
       1. Ten Boom, Corrie. 2. Christian biography—Netherlands. I. Title.
BR1725.T35M67 2004
269′.2′092—dc22   2004002862

Original Scriptures quoted by Corrie ten Boom are quoted from an original Dutch translation from the Hebrew and Greek and are not, therefore, identical to any of our English versions, although they are probably closest to the King James Version. In some cases, however, the author has changed Miss ten Boom's wording to the New International Version (NIV) in order to make it more easily understood by modern readers. Unless otherwise indicated, all other Scripture quotations are taken from the HOLY BIBLE, NEW INTERNATIONAL VERSION®, NIV® copyright © 1973, 1978, 1984, by International Bible Society. Used by permission of Zondervan. All rights reserved.

Scripture marked KJV is taken from the King James Version of the Bible.

Scripture marked PHILLIPS is taken from The New Testament in Modern English, revised edition—J. B. Phillips, translator. © J. B. Phillips 1958, 1960, 1972. Used by permission of MacMillan Publishing Co., Inc.

Scripture marked TLB is taken from The Living Bible © 1971. Used by permission of Tyndale House Publishers, Inc., Wheaton, IL 60189. All rights reserved.

Scripture marked RSV is taken from the Revised Standard Version of the Bible, copyright © 1946, 1952, 1971 by the Division of Christian Education of the National Council of the Churches of Christ in the USA. Used by permisson.

For those interested, the centuries-old house containing the hiding place is now a museum.

For more information visit www.CorrietenBoom.com

For Carey, with all my love

10/30

LIFE LESSONS
from the
HIDING PLACE

Other Books by Pam Rosewell Moore:

The Five Silent Years of Corrie ten Boom
Safer than a Known Way
When Spring Comes Late: Finding Your Way
   through Depression

With her husband, Carey Moore:
If Two Shall Agree, later published as *What Happens When Husbands and Wives Pray Together?*

Contents

Acknowledgments

I would first like to express my grateful appreciation to the Corrie ten Boom House Foundation in Haarlem, the Netherlands, and to the Billy Graham Center Archives in Wheaton, Illinois, U.S.A., for their permission to quote from the Ten Boom family letters and other documents. Some of the references have been printed earlier in various of Corrie ten Boom's more than twenty books of past decades, but the above two organizations hold the original material. In addition, a few of the letters are from my personal archives.

The excellent Dutch book *De Eeuw van mijn Vader* (My Father's Century) by Geert Mak was very helpful to me in describing the history, culture and people of the Netherlands in chapters 2 and 3.

I deeply appreciate the contributions made to this book by many family members, friends and professional contacts. These include my sister, Sylvia Baker, who helped me develop the concept; Terry Bensmiller, my research assistant; and Jane Campbell, Grace Sarber and Stephanie Vink, my editors.

Invaluable help was also given to me by Dr. Michael E. Williams, dean of the College of Humanities and Social Sciences and professor of history, Dallas Baptist University and by Dr. Ronald D. Rietveld, professor of history, California State University, Fullerton.

The Power
of a Good Story

One evening in 2001, a handful of children from a Christian school in Stalybridge, a small town in the north of England, performed a short play based on Corrie ten Boom's life. The setting was a simple school hall. As the boys and girls acted their parts, a hush descended on the parents and friends in the audience. The riveted attention in the room went beyond what would normally be expected of proud parents watching their children act. When the play ended, several parents commented on the story.

A mother exclaimed, "What a powerful story! I was so moved by it."

One father said, "I want to see it again; it was so good."

What makes this story powerful?

☙

Robert Pickle came to visit me one day from east Texas. He was one of the biggest men I have ever seen. I am fairly tall, but the broad-shouldered biker loomed above me. He was middle-aged and wore a ponytail and a thick black jacket studded with silver. Robert wanted to tell me how the story of Corrie ten Boom changed his life completely. While in prison, he was given a copy of *The Hiding Place*. Although he was not normally given to reading, Robert picked up the book and became engrossed in the story. Skeptical at first, he went on to read Corrie's *Tramp for the Lord*.

"There is nothing you can think of that I have not been guilty of," Robert told me, "but after I read those books I asked the Lord Jesus Christ to be my Savior. I gave Him all my life. He has changed me and given me a ministry to prisoners." Robert Pickle told his story with passion and joy, expressing his love for and gratitude to Corrie ten Boom.

How did a woman he had never met have such a strong influence on the hardened heart of Robert Pickle?

Diagnosed with bipolar disorder and later with clinical depression, Cindy suffered mental anguish for decades. She read *The Hiding Place* and said, "God has given me a second chance. He collects our tears. There are always tears in the heart when one is sad. Our wonderful Lord is deeper than the deepest pit in this fallen world. He is my Hiding Place."

Mindy told me how one story from Corrie's life helped her regain peace. It was the story of Corrie's meeting with one of her former tormentors at a speaking engagement in Germany shortly after World War II. The former guard from Ravensbrück concentration camp asked Corrie to forgive him for the way he had treated her and her dying sister, Betsie.

"And she forgave him," said Mindy. "This had a huge impact on me because at the time I read *The Hiding Place* I was personally dealing with serious issues of unforgiveness. Corrie taught me how to forgive, and I did forgive."

❧

Gail was a young mother with three preschoolers when she first heard Tante Corrie's story. Her husband supported her fully and helped her during all the hours he was not at his job, but it still seemed to Gail that life was filled with diapers, baby bottles, cleaning and seldom a good night's sleep. "My life was the Lord's," she said, "but deep inside I yearned for fresh inspiration for my walk with Christ. I found the model I was seeking in *The Hiding Place*. Strangely, in my twenties, I found this much older, never-married woman's story to be one that lifted my heart and brought richness and purpose to my ordinary, daily steps. She gave me a completely new perspective on life."

❧

Melody told me, "As a single woman I have always been challenged by how Corrie ten Boom lived so fully for Christ and did not settle into bitterness or hopelessness or self-pity. As I get older, I find myself often looking to those who have gone before me, and through them God says to me, 'Keep walking in faith, in the direction of hope. I am faithful. You can trust Me.'"

❧

Thousands more have their own stories. And most of them have never met Corrie ten Boom, let alone have the insights into her life and death that I, as her companion for the last seven years of her life, was allowed to receive.

Many concentration camp survivors have written autobiographies. What makes the story of *The Hiding Place* so powerful? Why does Tante Corrie's life have such unusual and lasting influence? The question intrigues me as much now as it did on that night in East Africa in the mid-1960s when, unknowingly, I was about to take part in her story.

one

Meeting Tante Corrie

It was during an evening meeting in tropical East Africa that I first heard her name. The year was 1966.

In my early twenties, I was working as a volunteer assistant for the Anglican Church of the Province of East Africa and had been invited to attend a nondenominational prayer meeting in a suburb of Nairobi, Kenya. Crickets chirped loudly outside. This was still a novel sound to me. I had never heard it in my home country of England. Nor had I ever before caught the sweet, heavy scent of the white and waxy frangipani flower that drifted through the wide open yet iron-barred window of the single-story suburban home where the prayer meeting was taking place.

Dozens of missionaries, men and women, filled that warm living room. Many of them described their work and asked for prayer. Seated at the back of the room, I kept quiet. I had never been one to speak up in public. But in my inner self I joined in the enthusiasm and prayers of the group.

Near the front of the room a middle-aged lady in a floral-printed frock raised her hand and stood up. "I would like to ask for prayer for Corrie ten Boom," she said. "She is in her mid-seventies now and has recently spent many months in Uganda. Her doctor had prescribed a sabbatical rest for her. But now she has resumed her world journeys."

I had never heard of Corrie ten Boom, but it seemed to me that the words of the woman in the floral dress were received with a kind of reverence, as if this elderly Corrie ten Boom were a legend in her own lifetime. I was intrigued. Not wanting to ask who she was, I listened interestedly as several missionaries volunteered experiences they had shared with her. From these reports, I was able to assemble my first impressions of the life and work of this Dutch missionary evangelist who had hidden Jewish people in her home in Holland during the Second World War and had been imprisoned by the Nazis for doing so. I also ascertained that after her release she had traveled the world for twenty years telling how she had proven God's love to be stronger than the deep darkness of Ravensbrück concentration camp and had learned to forgive those who had caused the deaths through imprisonment of her father, sister, brother and nephew. Inexplicably I was drawn to this old lady and her story. As the group prayed for her, I felt grateful I had been invited to the prayer meeting.

A chorus from the cricket choir greeted me as I left the house in that Nairobi suburb. *I would like to know more about Corrie ten Boom*, I said to myself. *I wonder if she has written any books about her work.*

First Impressions of Tante Corrie

In August 1968, the summer after my return to England from that short-term assignment in Africa, a friend invited me to go with her to a mission conference comprised of Dutch and English young people. It was to be held in the town of Matlock, Derbyshire, a beautiful, hilly part of north central England.

"Corrie ten Boom is one of the Dutch speakers," said my friend. I knew the name sounded familiar. Then it was as if I heard again the cricket chorus outside the suburban East African house a couple of years earlier, and I remembered the elderly lady who had saved Jewish lives in the Second World War. Recalling my intrigue about her story and curious to learn more about her, I traveled with my friend to Matlock and found myself part of the most unusual conference I had yet attended.

For one thing, there did not seem to be many halfhearted Christians among the fifty English and fifty Dutch young people. And for another thing, these Dutch were so different from the average English young person with whom I had grown up. They looked different; many of them were above the average English height, and they were mainly fair-haired and long-limbed. They also acted differently in that they spoke more loudly than I had been taught to speak. And they laughed a lot and heartily. I found this contrast with the more circumspect and cautious approach of the British a bit daunting.

One morning during the five-day conference, for example, it was discovered that about half the participants had contracted food poisoning from the meal the night before. I was fortunate to escape the affliction but not the frank questioning of a young Dutchman with whom several others and I sat at the half-empty breakfast table.

"Have you diarrhea?" he inquired with apparent interest as we began breakfast.

From the beginning of my acquaintance with them, I could see that there was no beating about the bush with the Dutch. On the whole they seemed to be honest, friendly, noisy, unpretentious, straightforward and opinionated. And I really liked them.

A Dutchman known as Brother Andrew was the main speaker. Also called "God's smuggler," he had a powerful message about what he called "the Suffering Church" under communism in Eastern Europe and the Soviet Union. He challenged us Western Christians to personal involvement, whether that meant taking Bibles and other help behind the Iron Curtain, giving or praying.

But his main emphasis was on going, whatever the personal cost or danger involved. I learned that he had carried out a Bible-smuggling mission from the Netherlands since 1955.

Soon it was Corrie ten Boom's turn to speak. She was 77 years old and physically strong-looking with a chin that can be well described as determined. Her height was about the same as mine—five foot seven. As I contemplated her size, I thought of the description on the army uniform my father was issued in England in the Second World War. "Slightly Portly" was the diplomatic British army description of Jim Rosewell's size. Not "Portly" or "Large," just "Slightly Portly." This phrase certainly described Tante (Aunt) Corrie, as the Dutch contingent referred to her. Just back from working in Asia, she was tired and always surrounded by people. I do not remember being introduced to her at that conference and had no idea that her life and mine would one day be closely bound together.

As I had learned was characteristic of the Dutch, Corrie ten Boom's messages during the five days of that conference were delivered with no sentiment or emotionalism. She just gave us the facts as she had experienced them.

"There is no pit so deep, the love of God is not deeper still," she said, speaking of her imprisonment in a concentration camp.

"We do not know when the Lord Jesus will return, but we do not know of one moment when He may not return. Are you ready? Have you forgiven your enemies? There was a time when I could not forgive those who had been so cruel to me and to my dying sister, Betsie. But God has taught me how to forgive.

"The Lord Jesus is coming again soon," she told us young people. "Are you obeying the Lord? Are you His ambassador?

"The Lord Jesus has promised to return. And He will. It may be very soon. In the meantime, are you taking hold of all the riches God has given us in Jesus Christ? We so often live like paupers when we are really children of the King of kings."

During that first week of August 1968 I heard Corrie ten Boom speak for the first time on the truths that formed the basis of her work and life. Later I was to hear the same consistent messages hundreds of times.

As the conference in the beautiful Peak District progressed, I noticed something in Corrie that went beyond the straightforward, frank and honest approach I had already noted in the Dutch participants—something harder to define. Her words seemed to carry an impressive authority and were delivered with unusual energy and dynamo. I felt rather intimidated by her powerful personality. But at the same time, observing her interaction with the young people through our five days together, I saw her love for them and their loving and interested response to her. She extended the same love with the same results to the conference leaders, the cooks, cleaners and gardeners as well. And I could not help noticing that every time Corrie ten Boom entered a room or took part in conversations, she was immediately the center of attention. It did not seem that she sought this. It simply happened.

A Surprise Invitation

As the conference drew to its close, I received a surprise invitation. Brother Andrew, whose book *God's Smuggler* had been released the previous year, told the group that he needed help. In response to that book, a large amount of correspondence in English arrived weekly at his ministry headquarters in Holland—mainly from American readers. He had even brought some items needing attention to the conference, and I volunteered to help him take care of them. Soon he asked if I would come to the town of Ermelo in central Holland, where his mission was based, to assist him. All the other team members were Dutch, and he wanted somebody whose first language was English to deal with the hundreds of inquiries being generated by the new book. I was free to go, having recently resigned from a temporary secretarial position, so I agreed to join him and his team in Holland for what

I thought would be a short time—perhaps three weeks. Little did I know my stay was to be much longer than that.

To Holland

After the conference ended, I said good-bye to my new friends, some of whom I would meet again in Holland. Returning to my family home in Hastings in East Sussex on the south coast of England, I packed my suitcase and took the cross-channel ferryboat to a port in Belgium, then a train to Holland. Before it stopped at Utrecht, a main railway junction, the train had introduced me to a land whose history, culture and people I was soon to love deeply. The landscape was orderly, green and flat with plenty of well-planned, open country areas between the cities. And forever remarkable to me, it was diffused with a clear and beautiful light.

I knew that Holland, although small, was one of the most densely populated countries in the world. From my seat in the train I saw that most of the cars the Dutch drove were small. Nearly all of the houses seemed small, too. They were mainly very clean and inviting. Most front room curtains were drawn back, and I was offered clear views into family living rooms, sometimes with many occupants, through high and wide polished windows.

I changed trains at that large junction and took a slower one that traveled in a north-easterly direction toward the small town of Ermelo, where Brother Andrew had said he would be waiting for me. To my relief, he was. We shook hands and observed each other briefly. Andrew (not his real name) was dressed in slacks and a casual shirt. His build was slight, his hair brown, his voice quiet. I contrasted his bearing with the loud and boisterous Dutch people I had met at the conference. *Perhaps it is easier for Andrew to keep anonymous in the Eastern European countries he visits,* I thought. He would be less conspicuous in those places than if he were tall and fair. As he shook my hand he studied me, a 23-year-old woman with dark brown hair, brown eyes and fair skin. I was wearing a

1960s minidress and Dr. Scholl's wooden sandals, which clacked noisily.

"Welkom in Holland, Pam," he said in his warm and charming way. As we hoisted my luggage into an oversized gray car—*Why such a large car for a missionary in a country of mainly small cars?* I asked myself—Brother Andrew explained he would drive me first to his home. He and his wife, Corry, had four children with a fifth on the way. We drove through quiet, tree-lined streets, and after reaching a busier street Brother Andrew stopped outside a house with a pointed red roof. Here Corry welcomed me, and then God's Smuggler led me up two flights of steps, the second of which was a steep, short, ladder-like staircase to the third floor—the attic under the pointed roof. It had been converted into an office and was large enough to contain four desks with chairs, typewriters and a few bookshelves and filing cabinets. The setup became even more fascinating when through the back window I saw a couple of station wagons parked on the property. Three large cars in one family? I also saw a medium-sized shed.

"We keep Bibles in the various languages of Eastern Europe in that shed," he told me. "And these cars belong to our mission. You may have noticed that they are larger than the average car in Holland, but they need to be. On our journeys to Eastern Europe we take as many Bibles as we can pack into them."

The intrigue was mounting. Was a dangerous international smuggling ministry really being carried out from this ordinary house in this fairly small town? I wanted to know more.

We descended the steep staircase, and I said farewell to Corry and the children. I supposed I would be back the next day to start my duties.

Brother Andrew then drove me to a small town nearby named Harderwijk, where he had arranged for the rental of two rooms in the little home of an elderly Dutch midwife, Miss Jo de Graaf. She spoke no English and I as yet no Dutch, but from the beginning we liked and understood each other. As he took leave, Brother Andrew told me that one of his team members would pick me up and take me to the office in the morning. And then he said, "Here you are. You will want to read this book to find out what our work is all about." And he handed me *God's Smuggler*.

My new landlady showed me to my bedroom. It was quiet, with a large picture window overlooking the backyard. The walls were white and so were the ceiling, sheets, pillowcases and candlestick bedspread. My room was comfortingly clean and inviting. I made myself ready for bed, propped myself up on pillows and started one of the most fascinating journeys of my life up to that time.

I do not remember how long I read that night, but *God's Smuggler* transported me to another world. I learned of the 1955 beginning of Brother Andrew's mission to Communist countries, of God's provision for his family, of his learning to listen to and obey the Holy Spirit. As the story progressed I was caught up into the fast-moving adventure of Bible smuggling. It sounded rather risky. I wanted to help by carrying out administrative work in the Dutch headquarters. I also wondered with a certain apprehension if in the future I would be invited to make journeys to any of those mysterious lands behind the iron curtain.

Beginning Work

As I began work the next day there were lesser mysteries to uncover. "Why is this country known by two names?" was one of my first questions to my co-workers. They told me that the country's official name, the Netherlands, refers to the low-lying nature of the country (*nether* meaning "low"). The name Holland is frequently used instead of the Netherlands, but it actually refers to the two western coastal provinces, North and South Holland, which have played an important role in the country's history.

And why were the language and the people of the country called Dutch? I learned that the noun derives from the word *Deutsch*, meaning "German." Europe was widely inhabited by Germanic and other tribes for countless centuries, and the German influence is still evident in the name of its language.

Another question I put to my new colleagues had to do with Dutch surnames. Brother Andrew's surname, which he did not publish for the sake of the Christians in Eastern Europe, had two words in its prefix. And then there was *Ten Boom*. I knew that *Boom* meant *tree*, but what did the prefix *Ten* mean, and why did I sometimes see the first letter T written in upper case and sometimes in lower?

Ten, it turned out, means "to the" in old Dutch. In Dutch grammar, when the word *Ten* stands alone, as it does when one refers, for instance, to the *Ten Boom* family, the first letter of the surname is capitalized. When the surname is combined with a Christian name, or family title such as Betsie *ten Boom* or Father *ten Boom*, lowercase is used for the first letter of the surname. Being a perfectionist in nature, I wanted to learn Dutch quickly and correctly and colloquially, but my unpretentious and down-to-earth new friends soon put me in my place, often laughing at my mistakes. They were kind and helpful, however, and eventually I learned their language—and to take myself less seriously.

Acclimating to Dutch Life

A couple of months after arriving in Holland I purchased a bike and pedaled my way to work and back each day, but for my first six weeks in the country in that autumn of 1968 I rode the bus because it rained incessantly. There was not one day when the sun appeared.

"Pam, you must make sure that you have plenty of sunshine inside when you live in Holland," said my new boss, "because there is not much outside."

My stay in Holland was to last more than seven years, during which time I came to love Holland and its people deeply. I made new friends and was often invited to team members' homes for meals, where I entered into a delightful Dutch state called *gezelligheid*. There is no translation for that word. *Coziness* is perhaps the nearest English word, but that does not capture *gezelligheid* at all. The dictionary says it means "companionable, convivial, sociable, clubbable and pleasant," but it is much more. It is togetherness in a deep, trusting, open, safe and enjoyable way. Coffee and cookies, low lights, flowers and laughter often accompany it. There are so many Dutch people that it is impossible for them to get away from each other. A person cannot be *gezellig* alone.

But being single, I was often alone. There were bike rides on Sunday afternoons on the trails in the woods just outside Harderwijk. It was exhilarating. I rode there in all seasons, autumn being my favorite. There were also many times when I left my lodgings and Miss de Graaf on Sunday afternoons and rode my bike a short distance to the dike and the low-lying polder lands beyond. Rows of tall and slender trees acted as windbreaks along the road to the polder and on the polder itself—trees that, along with grass plantings, stabilized the land so recently reclaimed from the sea. It was often very windy there, and when the wind was against me I leaned closer to the handlebars and kept going as quickly as I could pedal.

I persevered in my work, too. It was fulfilling, very busy, youth-oriented and adventurous. Eventually it did include several visits to Eastern Europe, where I had encounters with the persecuted Church that changed the way I looked at life. I was to learn many things from the Dutch and East European Christians, including how to pray so as to get what you ask. And I spent much time thinking on such things as the ethics of smuggling. Of course, the years contained disappointments and loneliness and some sadness. Life always does. But although there were many rainy days, it seemed to me there were a lot more days when that beautiful light appeared.

My First Encounter with Tante Corrie

But I must return to the time when my Dutch adventure was just beginning.

"One of the first things I want you to do," Brother Andrew told me upon my arrival in the Netherlands, "is to help my friend Corrie ten Boom."

He told me that the American authors John and Elizabeth Sherrill, co-writers of *God's Smuggler*, were now writing a book with Tante Corrie. It was not yet named, but work had begun. Hours of interviews with the writers and their subject had been audiotaped, and a typist was needed to transcribe them.

"I have volunteered you," said Brother Andrew.

And so my first personal encounter with Corrie ten Boom came to pass. She was usually absent from her home country on world journeys—her favorite title of the several ascribed to her by her friends was "Tramp for the Lord." But she spent several months in Holland during that autumn of 1968, mainly for the purpose of working on the new book. Her temporary residence was a borrowed apartment in the town of Soestdijk, about 45 minutes' drive from Brother Andrew's mission base.

As I traveled from my lodgings in Harderwijk to Tante Corrie's residence on that first misty, mellow autumn day, I looked forward to what promised to be an interesting undertaking. But I also felt rather apprehensive. This was the lady whose powerful presence I had found rather overwhelming at the mission conference in England two months before. Self-confidence had never been a strong point with me. And this lady seemed so very confident. I knew I had much to learn about the culture of the Dutch, and I certainly had never worked closely with Americans—or writers of any nationality for that matter—so the prospect of working with John and Elizabeth Sherrill was daunting as well. Would I be able to complete this assignment in a satisfactory way? I thought, *There must be many others more capable than I of helping with the production of a book.*

I arrived at Tante Corrie's lodgings, which were in a beautifully appointed apartment owned by a member of the Dutch nobility who was working in Israel and had made her home available to Corrie. My fears were put to rest quickly as I was welcomed so warmly. Blue, discerning eyes looked into my brown ones. I noted the healthy, olive-toned skin and the silver and gray hair arranged around a doughnut-shaped roll on the crown of her head.

"Come in, child," she said, "and let's have a talk. The Sherrills will be arriving soon. We will all travel together to Vught. That was the first concentration camp where Betsie and I were imprisoned. My co-authors want to be sure about the site of the camp and its surroundings and how it looked in 1944."

During the few minutes we had together before the arrival of her American friends, I was immediately drawn into Tante Corrie's world. We drank a cup of coffee, ate cookies made with butter and took each other in. It was *gezellig*.

"I am so glad you are going to help us with this book," she said, somehow conveying the assurance that I was a vital part of its birth.

A little later, as Tante Corrie, Elizabeth, John and I were driven to Holland's most southerly province and the site of the concentration camp, I watched the swiftly passing trees all dressed in gold, red, brown and yellow and reflected on the coffee time of half an hour before. Corrie ten Boom may have done courageous things during the war, traveled the world for decades, addressed hundreds of thousands of people and possessed a very powerful presence, but she certainly knew how to make an individual feel important and valuable. She had talked as if I were indispensable to her current project. And I believed her!

Beginning Work with Tante Corrie

We soon arrived at the site of the concentration camp, and I began to witness the care and determination with which the Sherrills recorded the facts of Corrie ten Boom's incarceration and, indeed, whole life story. At one point they asked Tante Corrie to describe how the tree-lined avenue on which we were walking had looked on the night in 1944 when she and her sister were brought to the camp.

"Corrie," said John Sherrill, "you told us that when you and Betsie were brought here soldiers stood near the trees on each side of this avenue. Where were the soldiers exactly—in the trees, or beside the trees? And those floodlights you told us were shining on you—were they in the trees or between the trees?"

"I don't remember," Corrie responded with no hesitation and with emphasis, unwilling to unlock memories of her wartime experiences. They were clearly hard for her to recall, but she stated that fact very honestly. This forceful personality was not afraid to show her fears and vulnerability.

During the coming months of the writing of the book, however, she made herself remember. I transcribed many tapes, and when *The Hiding Place* was published in 1971 it was fascinating to see how the skillful blending of such details as soldiers and trees with the element of danger for the Ten Boom family and the rescue of the Jewish people made this a book about which many still say, "I could not put it down."

Brother Andrew's work expanded, and so did the number of co-workers. We moved from the attic office under the pointed roof to a much larger headquarters, which housed more vehicles, Bibles and Christian book supplies in the various East European languages. An increasing number of people for whom English was their first language joined the team. I was no longer the only person who dealt with the continuing correspondence.

Asked to Be Tante Corrie's Companion

After I had worked with Brother Andrew for seven years, Corrie invited me to become her companion. Her Dutch companion of nearly nine years, Ellen, was soon to marry an American minister. I wondered how I, by now a rather independent Englishwoman in my early thirties, could possibly blend my lifestyle with that of a determined Dutch lady more than fifty years my senior. Was I cut out to be a companion? I did not think I was the type.

Deciding to accept Tante Corrie's invitation to an interview, however, I left Brother Andrew's headquarters on a March day in 1976 and drove to Overveen, a suburb of her hometown of Haarlem. She had a house there that had been her base since the previous year. A bunch of yellow tulips, a gift for Tante Corrie, lay in the passenger seat of the small, French, yellow-green car I was driving. As I entered the ancient city of Haarlem above which rose the roofs of the St. Bavo Dutch Reformed Church, also called the Great Church, I could not help but reflect on what had happened there. I thought of the small house lying almost in the shadow of that church on a street named Barteljoris where, more than thirty years before, Corrie ten Boom and her family were arrested for their part in saving Jewish lives.

Light rain was falling as I entered Juliana Avenue, where I would find Tante Corrie's home and headquarters. The wind blows across the Netherlands on most days, and this day was no exception. The cyclists on the bicycle paths on each side of the avenue had their heads down, those on the right side battling into the wind and rain from the nearby North Sea.

Pulling up to the curb as near as possible to house number 32, I parked the car. A short walk took me through part of the tree-lined street with its large and well-kept houses. The street was clean and neat in spite of its fairly heavy traffic. As I turned in at 32 Juliana Avenue, I noticed that the front yard had no gate. Dutch houses normally did. I later learned that since her imprisonment, Tante Corrie did not like to be shut in.

I rang the front doorbell and a few seconds later, Ellen de Kroon, Tante Corrie's companion, let me in.

I stepped into an atmosphere of peace and acceptance. I had experienced this several times before on visits to Tante Corrie over the years in whatever house she might have temporary residence. And from reports I heard, nearly everybody felt the same at her house—peaceful and welcome. Needed even.

Ellen welcomed me and said, "Let me take your coat."

She was tall and blond and, having seen her in action many times previously, I knew Ellen was a very able woman. Depending on the travel circumstances, her job responsibilities included, among many other tasks, those of chauffeuse, cook, cleaner, speaking schedule organizer, nurse, public speaker and counselor to many. She dealt with thousands of people and always tried her best to see that Tante Corrie got enough rest.

As she led me to the bottom of the stairs, Ellen explained that on the advice of her doctor Tante Corrie, then nearly 84, had recently begun to take one rest day each week. On this day of my visit, she was resting in her room on the second floor of the house.

"Tante Corrie is waiting for you. You know the way to her room, don't you?" asked Ellen. "Go on up, and I will bring tea in a little while."

I had visited this house before and did know the way. Clutching the yellow tulips, I climbed the steep staircase with slight trepidation but also with a sense of mounting adventure.

That Is Settled!

How on earth does Ellen do all those tasks and at the same time provide almost constant companionship to Tante Corrie? I asked myself. I did not know how the coming interview would turn out, but I was certain that I could not fulfill all of Ellen's roles as companion to Tante Corrie, should this elderly lady ask me to take her place. I was not a nurse, and Corrie's doctor had told me that her heart was not strong. I did not like cooking or driving, and I had a reserved personality, which might make dealing with thousands of people rather difficult. And although I had deep respect for Tante Corrie, I could hardly imagine being in this strong personality's presence 24 hours a day for an open-ended time.

Reaching the landing I knocked on her bedroom door, and Corrie ten Boom's firm and clear alto voice invited me to come inside. Entering her bright, fresh, colorful bedroom, I found her sitting up in bed wearing pale yellow nylon pajamas. The bedspread was covered with books, notebooks and writing implements, and her Bible was at her side. *This elderly lady may be resting her body,* I thought, *but she is not resting her mind.* We greeted each other with smiles, and I handed her the yellow tulips.

She thanked me, deposited the flowers on a bedside table and invited me to sit down. Drawing a comfortable chair closer to her bed, I looked into her blue eyes and thought how good she looked. Her silver-gray hair was not arranged in the usual roll around her head on this, her rest day. Fine and straight, it was neatly combed and rested on her shoulders, somehow making her look rather vulnerable. These observations did not last longer than a few seconds, however, because, characteristically, Tante Corrie came straight to the point.

"Well, child, what has the Lord told you?"

"I am willing to help you, Tante Corrie . . ." I ventured, by way of a start.

"Praise the Lord! That is settled then!"

But for me it was not settled at all. I had not even finished the sentence. I had been going to say, "I am willing to help you until you have found a more suitable companion."

Tante Corrie began to tell me about her plans for the coming months, which included returning to the United States, where most of her work in latter years had taken place. "I have so many opportunities in America," she said. "*The Hiding Place* has been read by thousands of people. And now there is a new movie giving the story of the book. I have many more invitations to speak than I can accept."

She went on to tell me that among many other appointments, she was soon to speak at a sunrise service in Florida, work for several days with a pastor in Brooklyn, be interviewed for a television program in Toronto and receive an honorary degree from Gordon College in Massachusetts. After all this, she was to speak to prisoners in Chicago and Hawaii. At the same time she told me she would work on several writing projects, including a new book.

"The whole journey will take seven months," she stated matter-of-factly. "Do come with me to help me."

Seven months for a person in her mid-eighties. How ever would she get through it? How would I get through it? But I was beginning to catch her enthusiasm, and besides, it sounded like a good adventure.

"I'll go with you for the next seven months, Tante Corrie," I promised. My boss, Brother Andrew, knowing of her need for a new companion, had told me he would give me a leave of absence for several months to help his old friend Corrie, should she ask me.

Getting to Know Tante Corrie

Ellen joined us, bringing the tea, and we three spent a couple of hours talking about the travel itinerary and what my duties would be. While Ellen went to the kitchen to prepare supper and Tante Corrie took care of some items on her desk, I looked at the many items on the walls of her room. I had seen them briefly on a previous visit to this room, but now I could inspect them more closely. Tante Corrie obviously loved these objects and had hung many of them as closely as space permitted. Some were original oil or watercolor paintings, somehow kept safe in the War. Others were reproductions of works by old Dutch masters, including Rembrandt with his enchanting use of light. Other items on the wall included plaques on which were written Scripture texts of special meaning to her. Some were framed, and most were small. I read them all and was struck by one in particular. It was not particularly pretty, but it did stand out. It was a rectangular plaque without a frame. Its background was reddish pink with the words *Mijn tijden zijn in Uw hand*— "My times are in your hands"—written boldly in black. Underneath was the Scripture reference—Psalm 31:15.

Ellen produced a good meal in a short time, and after some more planning I took leave of them, turning the small, light-green car toward Harderwijk and home. As daylight dissolved to dusk I reached the last half of my journey where the lighter traffic allowed me to think about the events of the day. It looked as though I would be returning soon to Haarlem to accompany Corrie ten Boom on her journeys for seven months. Yet I did not feel as though I had been pushed into accepting her invitation to go with her. Although she had been quite sure that it was right for me to be her new companion and I was not so sure, I knew her well enough to know that she would not act presumptuously or force a decision on me.

What remarkable faith and trust in God Corrie has, I thought. *She is so sure about the work God has given her and how to carry it out. She lives close to Him, and her decisions have been proven right on countless occasions. She believes it is right for me to join her.* Although I did not share her certainty, I did feel a kind of peace about it. There was comfort in the fact that God always seemed to honor Tante Corrie's decisions.

I decided to leave things as they were for now and see what happened in seven months' time. In the meantime, perhaps I would gain insights into what made her the woman she was. What kinds of things had influenced the peaceful and purposeful life she was living? How could I learn to live like that?

A few weeks later, with Brother Andrew's blessing, I arrived again at Tante Corrie's front door, with two suitcases. We began our work together on April 1, 1976. Several days before our departure on April 6, Tante Corrie began packing for the long journey. Here I caught a glimpse of her very pragmatic side. We were in her bedroom and placed the suitcases on her low bed. For the first time I saw some of the things that the long years of traveling had taught her. It was of real importance to her that we be ready in plenty of time to prevent a last-minute rush. Between us we had seven pieces of luggage, including small and large cases. She asked me to count the luggage carefully as it was loaded at the airport and again upon arrival. We began by packing her items, and I noticed that she worked methodically, never pausing to ponder or worry that she might forget something important. Last of all, she packed a copy of the New Testament translation by J. B. Phillips right at the top of a small bag for easy access. Judging by its rather worn black cover, it looked as if it had accompanied her on many journeys.

At one point Tante Corrie packed a folded piece of shiny blue material with yellow threads hanging from it. I asked if it was some embroidery she was working on.

"No, child," she replied, her blue eyes alive with some secret, "this is what I call 'the crown.' You will see how I use it later." Saying no more, she slipped it into a cloth bag.

And so I left the Netherlands, the land I had grown to love so deeply, with its straightforward people, its language, poetry, history, the flat green lowlands on which the wind always blew and the mysterious light from the huge dome of a sky. And that short assignment, which I originally thought would last seven months, turned into seven years—time spent mainly in the United States.

From Travel to Rest

Tante Corrie traveled, wrote books, spoke at gatherings large and small and in February 1977 moved into a rented house in Placentia in Orange County, California. Her heart needed rest, but Tante Corrie disliked rest. It seemed to me she worked as hard as ever, although she did not travel as much as in previous years. She wrote several books, conducted telephone and letter correspondence, gave interviews and received many guests.

Eighteen months later, on August 23, 1978, I took tea to her room as I always did early in the morning. I knew I would find Tante Corrie propped up on her pillows, her J. B. Phillips translation of the New Testament open on her chest. The thick curtain on the big picture window facing east, which had shut out light during the night and early morning, would have been determinedly drawn back and Tante Corrie would be planning her day.

Teatime together was a time of quiet fellowship and prayer before each busy day began. We talked about the day before and the day lying ahead. The talks were always about people—ones she had worked with decades before, others she had met on her world journeys who were passing through Los Angeles, our neighbors and the children down the road, and the many unknown people who did not yet know the Lord Jesus. And we read the Scriptures together and prayed for those we discussed. It was perhaps the one part of the day when I could expect things to be the same as they had been the morning before.

But this day was different. For one thing, as I carried the tea tray along the corridor leading to her bedroom, I saw that all was dark inside. This was unusual, but I was glad she was sleeping in. She had complained of bad headaches in previous days.

I felt my way into the darkened room, put the tray down and extended my right hand to draw the heavy curtain. It pulled slowly back. Then I pulled on the rope that drew back the light green, filmy sheer.

I turned around and faced a completely different Tante Corrie from the one I had bid good night the evening before. She was conscious but looked very confused. I was so shocked that it seemed I froze in place for a few seconds. I greeted her, but there was no response. I ran to her and took her right hand. "Let's pray, Tante Corrie," I said. She immediately closed her eyes, and I asked the Lord to help her. Then I summoned an ambulance, and she was taken to the local hospital, where a stroke was diagnosed.

After a few weeks, Tante Corrie came home, but her brain was permanently damaged. She could not do the normal things we do with language—she was unable to speak, write or comprehend as she had before. Sometimes, but rarely, she managed a few words appropriate to the occasion. She never learned to write again. Those of us who helped her during the next five years became sure that there were times when she could comprehend, but we were unsure as to what degree and when.

It was a different Tante Corrie with whom I lived for the next five years, yet in spite of some pain and much discouragement, not a less resolute or consistent one. During what I call the five silent years that followed, in what seemed to be a very slow movement of time, I watched closely and I saw that Christianity really works. On April 15, 1983, her 91st birthday, Corrie ten Boom passed away at her rented home in Placentia, California.

Discovering the Heart of Tante Corrie

Corrie ten Boom's speaking and writing ministry reached hundreds of thousands of people, and in the years since her death the impact of her story has remained strong. She frequently told her audiences, "We are living in one of the darkest times of the history of the whole world." I wonder what she would think now. More than two decades after her death, the times appointed to you and me seem even darker. What can we discover about the heart of Corrie ten Boom that will help us to persevere with a better understanding of our own times—and with less fear and real victory?

I invite you to come with me on a journey into her story in which we will see afresh the kinds of things that influenced the peaceful and purposeful life Corrie lived.

We can learn from her how to put into practice the how-tos of faith that are essential to real Christian living in our times. We will discover things like:

- Learning to tell our own story
- How to maintain strong family relationships
- How to develop strong community relationships
- How to live a single life
- How to forgive our enemies
- How to get along with less
- The secret of simplicity

Corrie ten Boom told her story many times. And it was in the telling of that story that lives were changed. Deep within each human being is an ancient, profound desire for a good story. You and I have a story, too, without which every other Christian is the poorer. Perhaps in learning how Corrie told her story, we will learn how to tell our own stories as well—and in so doing we will affect our world in ways that only eternity will tell.

It was 1892 when Corrie's story began.

two

Corrie's Early Life and Influences

1892–1910

Corrie ten Boom was thoroughly Dutch, in large part a product of her time and her nation. As with each of us, the history, environment, spiritual, physical and social conditions of the country of her birth had indelible effects on her and on the story she told us.

The Holland into which she was born in Amsterdam on April 15, 1892, had enjoyed peace for decades—longer than most people could remember. This followed centuries of conquests, control, invasions, wars and raids by, for example, the Romans, Germanic tribes, Vikings, Hapsburgs, Spaniards, English and French. As a result of Napoleon's march across Europe, little Holland (14,103 square miles in area—the size of Massachusetts, Connecticut and Rhode Island combined) was incorporated into the French empire in 1810 and was ruled by Napoleon's followers.

Corrie's great-grandfather Gerrit ten Boom, a staunch Calvinist, lived in Napoleonic times. A master gardener on an estate, he lived and worked in the outskirts of Haarlem. Gerrit stood up to the Napoleonic government several times. On at least one occasion, after he had rallied the members of his Dutch Reformed Church to remember their true freedom as Dutch citizens and Christians, he was brought before the authorities. Had his influential employer not intervened he would probably have been sentenced to prison. Corrie's father, Casper, was proud of his grandfather Gerrit and told Corrie, "I am glad he was a real man."

Gerrit's influence on his grandson was evident more than one hundred years later. When people warned Casper, "Stop having Jews in your house—you will be sent to prison," he answered, "I am too old for prison life, but if that should happen, I would be honored to give my life for God's ancient people, the Jews."

And great-grandfather Gerrit's son Willem (Corrie's grandfather) also made a large contribution to the coming generations of Ten Booms. In 1844, while in his late twenties, he began a weekly prayer meeting for Israel, to "pray for the peace of Jerusalem." He had become part of a revival movement in the middle of the nineteenth century started by Willem Bilderdijk and Isaac Da Costa, a Jew of Portuguese descent who converted to Christianity. The influence of both these men on the Ten Boom family was profound. Father Casper ten Boom told Corrie that a picture of Da Costa always hung in the family home while he was growing up. (appendix 1 to this book further explains the influence of Isaac Da Costa on Corrie's grandfather Willem in regard to the Jewish people, for whose sake several of the Ten Booms would later lose their lives.)

Jewish people had found a refuge in Holland ever since the first Prince of Orange (of the Dutch royal family's House of Orange) delivered the country from Spanish rule in the seventeenth century. Holland became a land of freedom and security for oppressed people from many countries. The Jews settled mainly in Amsterdam and even called that city "the New Jerusalem."

Years later Corrie told her audiences: "We never know how God will answer our prayers, but we can expect that He will get us involved in His plan for the answers. If we are true intercessors, we must be ready to take part in God's work on behalf of the people for whom we pray."

"A Very Little, Weak Baby"

Corrie's mother, Cor ten Boom, kept a diary of sorts. Her entries were made once or twice a year, from 1887 until 1909. Her purpose was to keep notes about her children: "It seems to me it might be so nice for them, when they are grown up (the Lord sparing them) to read some things about themselves when they were small."

This is part of her entry on December 31, 1892:

What an eventful year we have had. At times it was so dark and difficult, but the Lord spared us for one another and we also received a very small baby, which we had been expecting in May, but which arrived a month early, on Good Friday. We will never forget the happenings of that day, the awful fear in those dark hours, our crying out to the Lord to spare me. The Lord heard and gave us a very little, weak baby, Corrie. Oh, what a poor little thing it was. It was nearly dead and looked bluish-white at birth. I never saw anything so pitiful. Nobody thought it would live.

Child of a Godly, Loving Marriage

Corrie was the fifth and youngest child of Casper and Cornelia ten Boom, known to each other and to their friends as Cas and Cor. Born in 1858, Cor was the seventh of the eight children of Arent Luitingh and his wife, Cornelia Frings. Shortly after the birth of the couple's eighth child, Anna, at the end of 1860, father Arent died at about fifty years of age, leaving his 42-year-old wife with a small store to manage in Amsterdam. As soon as they were old enough all the children worked to support the family.

When Cor was in her late teens, she and her youngest sister, Anna, taught in a kindergarten started by Jans, their resolute older sister. Jans then added a Sunday school, and it was here that Cor Luitingh met Casper ten Boom. The two of them found they had much in common, including the same birthday, May 18.

Their friendship grew, and one day when Cor decided to visit her grandmother in Harderwijk, Casper missed her so much that he followed her there the next day. In view of the limited means of transport, Cor must have realized there was more to Casper's being there than just a visit. Indeed, the next day he made a proposal of marriage to Cor. Their wedding took place on October 16, 1884.

About fifty years later, Corrie and her father visited Harderwijk, a fishing village on the Zuider Zee, Holland's inland sea, now reclaimed polder land. I can still hear Corrie tell the story:

> As we walked along the Bruggestraat, Father said: "This is where I proposed to your mother. There were cobblestones instead of pavement at that time, but many of the old houses and the sea gate are still the same." I asked him if Mother had said yes immediately. "No, not until the next day," he answered, "and I spent a very restless night waiting for that decision!"[1]

When Corrie asked him if he had ever regretted his decision to marry Mother his voice was firm. "Never! Until the last day of her life, I was just as much in love with your mother as I was on that day in Harderwijk. We did not have an easy life—we had many sorrows—but God led us by His extraordinary providence."[2]

The Watchmaker Ten Booms

Casper ten Boom was the eldest child of the second marriage of Willem ten Boom, whose first wife Geertruida died

Ten Boom Family, 1900 PHOTO COURTESY OF THE CORRIE TEN BOOM HOUSE FOUNDATION

of tuberculosis in 1856 after giving birth to thirteen children, most of whom also died of the same disease. Corrie's grandfather Willem was a watchmaker by trade, and in 1837 he set up shop in the city of Haarlem.

Casper followed his father's profession and established a business in Amsterdam, where each of his five children was born. In 1892, after the death of his father, Casper and his family moved to Haarlem where he took over his father's business at 19 Barteljorisstraat (Barteljoris Street). Since the full name of that street is a bit of a mouthful, the Ten Booms contracted their particular address to Beje, the Dutch spelling for the letters B and J—B for Bartel and J for Joris. This is pronounced *bay-yay* in Dutch. Actually, over the centuries there probably had been a corruption in the street's name. It is said that Bartel may really stand for Martel or *martyr*. Martyr Joris was put to death in the Dutch city of Dordrecht in 1558. Barteljorisstraat commemorates him and, to those who know the story, four other martyrs from number 19 nearly five hundred years later during World War II.

I am looking at a photograph taken in 1897 of Casper and Cor ten Boom's children—Betsie, Willem, Nollie and Corrie.

Betsie, Willem, Nollie, Corrie, 1897   PHOTO COURTESY OF THE CORRIE TEN BOOM HOUSE FOUNDATION

The children are facing the camera and are depicted in decreasing height. The oldest child, Betsie, is on the left. Twelve years old, she is wearing a white dress with big frilly sleeves and a high neckline. Her long brown hair is pulled back and a thick ringlet hangs over her left shoulder.

Next to her is brother Willem, wearing a white shirt and black jacket that seems too big for him. His black hair is cropped short. Like that of Betsie, his expression is enigmatic. The two were born within fifteen months of each other, and Willem is half a head shorter than Betsie.

The next step down is a longer one. Beside Willem is sister Nollie, wearing a white dress with a splendid, large ruffled collar and a wistful expression. A gap of three and a half years separated Willem and Nollie. Had he lived, their brother Hendrik would have filled the middle space in this line-up of the Ten Boom children. But he died at six months from "a terrible brain fever."

Then, at the far right we see the youngest child, five-year-old Corrie. She, too, is wearing something white, but time has faded the details of her clothing. She is looking into the camera with a most serious expression.

41

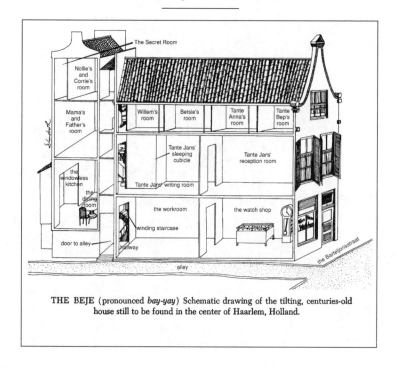

THE BEJE (pronounced *bay-yay*) Schematic drawing of the tilting, centuries-old house still to be found in the center of Haarlem, Holland.

The Beje

Five-year-old Corrie's home was near the marketplace that bordered the pre-Reformation St. Bavo Cathedral, the family's Dutch Reformed Church. It was then known as the Grote Kerk, the Great Church. The Beje itself, as the Ten Booms called their home, was actually two houses joined together. The first house was built in the 1400s. Like many of the ancient houses in Haarlem it was very small, with three stories, two rooms deep and one room wide. This was the house Father ten Boom inherited, and he soon found that it was too small for himself and Cor, their four children and Cor's three sisters—Bep, Jans and Anna—who one by one had joined the household. The three did not have the means to support themselves, although Tante Jans did have a small source of income, a pension as the widow of a minister.

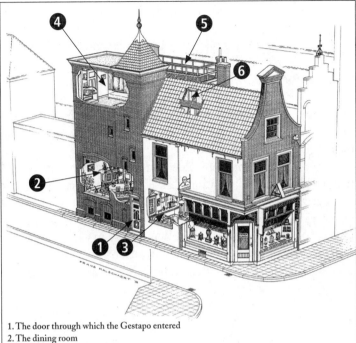

1. The door through which the Gestapo entered
2. The dining room
3. Father ten Boom's workshop
4. Corrie's bedroom, with its hiding place
5. The balcony on which those in hiding took fresh air
6. This location was once considered as a hiding place but was never used.

COURTESY OF THE CORRIE TEN BOOM HOUSE FOUNDATION

There was no question in Father ten Boom's mind that his wife's sisters should live with his family, but he knew he had to supply more space. He was able to purchase the very narrow house behind the existing home. A narrow alley separated the two houses, so Casper arranged for the houses to be joined by breaking through walls, building extra outside walls and adding a steep, winding staircase to join the two. Since the houses are on different levels, doorways issue out of the staircase at unusual intervals, and the family stepped up or down into a room, depending upon which part of the house they were entering or exiting.

To this day I find the house confusing. Perhaps the Nazis did, too, when they failed to find the secret room built to hide Jewish people. Behind a false wall in Corrie's small bedroom at the top of the house was an area about two feet wide and eight feet long. Entrance to the hiding place was gained by crawling through a wooden sliding panel at the back of the linen cupboard that was built into the false wall. It was professionally built with real bricks by a co-worker in the underground work. There was no hollow sound when the Nazis hammered on it or any other wall in the house, and even when the Ten Booms were led away to prison on February 28, 1944, it did not give up its secret.

Tante Bep, the children's oldest aunt, had never married and had a rather dour disposition. Tante Corrie always said that it was because she had worked as a governess all her life and had never had a home or family of her own. Tante Anna, also never married, was the youngest aunt. Being close in age, she and her sister Cor had always had a special relationship, and Anna had been with the family since Betsie's birth. The third aunt, widowed Tante Jans, was an evangelist, a strong-minded woman who took over most of the second floor of the house. The four children, Tante Anna and Tante Bep had their bedrooms upstairs on the third floor. Nollie and Corrie shared a room not quite ten feet by seven feet in size. Mother and Father slept in a small room on the second floor.

The Oval Table

The Beje's dining room was at the back of the house overlooking an alley. Lit by gas lamps, it was five steps higher than the watch shop but lower than Tante Jans' rooms. Its oval table was a place of much *gezelligheid*, that untranslatable Dutch word meaning fellow-feeling, comradeship, laughter and trust. Meals would consist of two *broodmaaltijden* (bread meals) each day and one other meal. The bread meals were simply that—bread with butter, thinly sliced cheese, sometimes thinly sliced meat, jam, milk and plain yogurt. The main, hot meal consisted primarily of vegetables—cabbage, for example, or peas, green beans, kale or beets—normally with a small amount of meat. And, without exception, potatoes.

At the oval table, which was usually covered by a black and red cloth, the Ten Booms read the Bible from various translations. Casper ten Boom wanted to broaden his children's thinking, and he held Bible studies in several languages simultaneously. While they studied the same passage, different family members read from Dutch, French, German, English, Hebrew and Greek Bibles.

During mealtimes they made plans, some of which must have been about their frequent travels and stays away from Haarlem and the Beje. They must have confided their hopes and dreams to each other, too, but on the simplest of levels they wanted to know what each family member had done that day. "Tell me every detail," Tante Corrie used to ask me when we lived together in California and I came home from a day away. "You stepped into the car. What happened next?"

Two recurring problems must have surfaced at times at the oval table—Father's financial difficulties and Mother's chronically delicate health. Father was a good watchmaker, but he had a hard time making ends meet in his household of nine, especially when he sometimes failed to send bills to customers whom he knew would find it hard to pay for his repairs.

In keeping with Victorian modesty Mother's health problems are not described in the family letters, but they necessitated frequent times of recuperation away from the city through most of the years of their marriage. Betsie, who suffered from a blood disease, was also often away convalescing, and Willem, Nollie and Corrie made many more journeys away from home than would have been normal for a family of their means. Because the family members wrote to each other almost every day during their times away, a rather remarkable record of their daily lives is preserved.

All accounts given in the many preserved letters between the Ten Boom children and their parents, aunts and friends are so full of love and admiration for each other that the family seems perfect! Since they were a normal family, this surely could not always have been the case, but there is little trace of disharmony in any letters or diaries, or in the stories Tante Corrie told me. Therefore, when John and Elizabeth Sherrill, writers of *The Hiding Place*, were looking for a way to describe life in the Beje that would reflect some of the tensions inevitably found in families (thus making them real), they were glad when they were finally able to say with relief, "We were delighted to find a few abrasive aunts!"

There was one serious disharmony, however. Mother's diary entry on New Year's Eve 1895 reads:

> Some very dark clouds have come up...it concerns my husband and his mother. That battle has been going on for such a long time. What a terrible thought—that a mother is not living in peace with her own children. . . . So many prayers have been offered for this very sad state of affairs. I only trust that the battle will not grow too heavy for my dear husband. He looks so unwell.

We do not know the end of that part of the story, but it seems that Casper's mother was permanently estranged from the family. Corrie never wrote about or spoke of her grandmother, Elisabeth Bel ten Boom (after whom Betsie was presumably named) in any of the papers I have studied, even though she lived and died in Haarlem.

Corrie's World in the 1890s

Looking outside their house, five-year-old Corrie would have seen a densely populated city with many houses the same shape and size as that of her family. Streets were narrow and houses tall, some of them leaning and many with distinctive gables. Most houses adjoined each other except at intersections of streets, alleys and canals.

One of the first paved roads in Holland ran the short distance between Haarlem and Amsterdam. It was less than four-and-one-half yards wide. A few times each day an automobile would be seen traveling down it.

From the Dutch census of 1899 we know that Holland had a population of about five million at the time of Corrie's birth. Three-quarters of the population lived and worked on the land. Many houses and farms built in the seventeenth or eighteenth centuries were still in daily use.

There is a well-known Dutch poem that describes Holland beautifully:

> When I think of Holland I see broad rivers moving very
>   slowly through endless lowlands
> And rows of very tall poplars that look like long feathers
>   standing on end. . . .[3]

Rivers, canals and other watercourses with their locks and sluice gates crisscrossed the flat Dutch landscape. Much of the land is below sea level, and the sea had always been the fiercest enemy of the lowlands. Disastrous floods mainly from the North Sea had caused untold numbers of deaths throughout the centuries. From the air the lowlands can be clearly seen for what they are—a very large delta.

Young Corrie's Holland continued a hurtling journey begun decades earlier. With the rest of Europe her little country moved frantically through and toward far-reaching and inexorable change. Between 1880 and 1914 nearly all the big towns underwent fast alteration—boulevards were built in the cities, along with squares, new housing districts, warehouses, museums, theaters and train stations. People slowly gained more free time, more convenience, better food and better education in hygiene.

The French elite gave a name to the years 1890–1914—*La Belle Époque* ("The Beautiful Time"). Freedom reigned throughout Europe, and new innovations such as electricity and cars were changing the continent rapidly. So were advances in medicine and welfare. But the increasingly comfortable changes of "The Beautiful Time" were mainly for the upper class. In Holland, more than a quarter of the population lived in housing consisting of just one room, even though there were often four, six or even eight people in a family. A high percentage of the people did not reach their fiftieth birthday. Every 45 minutes someone died of tuberculosis. Mother Cor's diary entries were full of prayers and pleadings that she and Casper might be able to "keep their children." She wrote about times when the children were so ill with diseases such as diphtheria, flu and scarlet fever that she could not see how they could live. She never referred to their future without saying "the Lord willing."

Corrie also used the expression "the Lord willing" quite often, and so did many Dutch Christians in the Calvinist tradition. They took very seriously the New Testament's admonition through James, "Listen, you who say, 'Today or tomorrow we will go to this or that city, spend a year there, carry on business and make money.' Why, you do not even know what will happen tomorrow. . . . Instead, you ought to say, 'If it is the Lord's will, we will live and do this or that'"(James 4:13–15).

Religious Changes

Corrie's family belonged to the Dutch Reformed Church, the state church in which Corrie was christened in July 1892. The Ten Booms were uncomplicated people who believed that Christians could know God personally and discover and follow His will. For them and many others in their day faith was not a theological construct but a daily, self-evident reality. Father ten Boom knew his Bible from cover to cover. He was widely read and always ready to discuss theological issues.

Father ten Boom was a Calvinist, but he did not live in a rigid theological system. Corrie was influenced greatly by him and by her church's theology. She, like him I believe, talked less about "the sovereignty of God" than about "my times are in His hands." Corrie wrote in 1976, "Father was not quarrelsome about his biblical beliefs, but he stood fast in theological debates. . . . I heard him speak frequently about predestination. I never quite understood what he meant, and one time I asked him, 'What is predestination?' He answered, 'The ground on which I build my faith is not in me, but in the faithfulness of God.'" She was to repeat that statement many times in the years that followed.

The census of 1899 tells us that only two percent of the population admitted to having no church affiliation. The Renaissance (1400s) and the Enlightenment (1700s), with the resulting new thinking and scientific discoveries, had caused differences in theological thought and had divided Protestant churches in Holland and across Europe.

Dr. Abraham Kuyper, journalist, pastor, statesman and strongly Orthodox theologian, was used by God to turn the Dutch people's dissatisfaction with modernity and liberalism into a strong mass movement. Although theologically conservative, Kuyper was a radical reformer socially and politically. He was the leader of the mainly rural conservative Dutch Christians whom he called the *kleine luiden* (the "little people"). In 1880 he founded the Free University of Amsterdam on theologically reformed principles. Kuyper's influence on the religious and national life of Holland from about 1870 until his death in 1920 and later was immense. He declared "the absolute sovereignty of God" and believed that the only true Holland was a Calvinistic Holland.

Kuyper and his followers wanted to take over the Dutch Reformed Church, but an attempt to seize power in 1886 was unsuccessful. A break with that church then occurred, and Kuyper became the leader of the *Gereformeerde* (Re-reformed) Churches. The theology of Kuyper's churches was that the promises of God were no longer made to the Jews, since they had rejected the Messiah. The Church, not the Jews, was now the recipient of the promises of God. The theology of Father ten Boom's church, on the other hand, emphasized the importance of the Jewish people and the restoration of the Jewish nation.

In 1901, when Corrie was nine years old, Abraham Kuyper became prime minister of the Netherlands. Although they remained in the Dutch Reformed Church, the Ten Booms were certainly influenced by him. "Father voted for him," noted Corrie decades later.

Kuyper began Christian schools throughout the nation. Corrie and her sister Nollie attended Haarlem's Christian school, of which their father was one of the founders.

Come as a Little Child

Corrie often told the story of the most important decision of her life, made in 1897. She has recorded this in books, films, videotapes and letters. These are her own words:

When I was five years old, I learned to read: I loved stories, particularly those about Jesus. He was a member of the Ten Boom family—it was just as easy to talk to Him as it was to carry on a conversation with my mother and father, my aunts or my brother and sisters. He was there.

One day my mother was watching me play house. In my little girl world of fantasy, she saw that I was pretending to call on a neighbor. I knocked on the make-believe door and waited . . . no one answered. "Corrie," said my mother, "I know Someone who is standing at your door and knocking right now."

Was she playing a game with me? I know now that there was a preparation within my childish heart for that moment; the Holy Spirit makes us ready for acceptance of Jesus Christ, of turning our life over to Him.

"Jesus said that He is standing at the door, and if you invite Him in He will come into your heart," my mother continued. "Would you like to invite Jesus in?" At that moment my mother was the most beautiful person in the whole world to me. "Yes, Mama, I want Jesus in my heart."

So she took my little hand in hers and we prayed together. It was so simple, and yet Jesus Christ says that we must all come as children, no matter what our age, social standing or intellectual background. When Mother told me later about this experience, I recalled it clearly.[4]

Early Signs of Corrie's Gifts

Mother's diary entries in the last years of the nineteenth century describe Betsie, Nollie and Willem as beautiful children who developed quickly. Corrie is depicted as a very sweet but ugly child, except for her large and beautiful blue eyes. Compared to her brother and sisters she was slow developing.

A few months before Corrie's tenth birthday in 1902, Mother ten Boom's diary gives us the first glimpse of a gift her daughter would later develop to such an extent that she would become one of the most influential women communicators God has given to the Church in our time. Her mother wrote, "Our 'baby,' Corrie, is the family's darling, particularly because of her lovely way of putting things into words. She is a surprise to everyone because of the way she talks, and she is so cute sometimes that it astonishes us."

Corrie was part of a family who loved life and lived it with passion, and this was evident in each of them—but especially in Corrie. Their hope and prayers for their queen and her baby serve as evidence of that.

The Ten Booms, like most other Christians, were strongly patriotic, but not at all nationalistic. They loved their queen and country. They offered many prayers for Wilhelmina, Queen of the Netherlands, because after years of her marriage to German Prince Hendrik the couple remained childless. Royal families still played a central role in international politics, and the people knew the lack of an heir to the throne of the Netherlands could have big political consequences, especially if the crown came to rest on the head of some distantly related German. In 1902, Queen Wilhelmina became critically ill with typhus, and some feared that before too long Holland might become part of Germany.

But at last, in 1908, the queen was expecting. The prayers of the Ten Booms and their friends became even more urgent. Betsie, away from home for recuperation from an illness, wrote on April 17 to the Beje, "Everyone is waiting for the prince here, too!" The Netherlands had already had two long-reigning queens, so the hope of a prince was strong.

Betsie, Nollie, Corrie, 1905   PHOTO COURTESY OF THE CORRIE TEN BOOM HOUSE FOUNDATION

Tante Jans, writing from the Beje on April 28, said, "At 10 a.m. this morning we received the news from The Hague that things had 'begun.' Toward sunset the great event is expected."

Willem wrote to the Beje the same evening: "Dear Father, Mother, Sisters, Aunts . . . it gradually looks as if my joyful expectation, together with that of the whole nation, will be fulfilled."

At 7:30 a.m. on Friday, April 30, seventeen-year-old Corrie learned the news of the safe arrival of Princess Juliana through a telephone call. She wrote to Betsie:

> I shall never forget how I felt when I heard it was a princess. I shouted, 'A Princess!!!' I quite forgot to be quiet and walk softly, which is always best before 8:00 a.m. I even wanted Tante Jans to get out of bed, but she had not slept yet, although she did not sleep much afterward because nobody kept quiet.
>
> In just a few minutes, flags were flying everywhere, except on the church tower, because of which Tante Anna did not dare to believe it. We all went and stood in front of the mayor's

house, where we sang the "Wilhelmus" [the Dutch national anthem] as loudly as we could.

Corrie's response shows her never-ending enthusiasm for life, so evident in her obvious joy at the arrival of a baby girl, even though they had hoped for a prince. It is an example of her rather mischievous sense of humor, revealed by the teasing reference to her rather daunting Tante Jans.

Her wonderful sense of humor, as well as her merciful heart, is evident in other letters. Earlier in that month of April, for example, in a letter to Betsie, Corrie makes reference to the family cat. But first she teases Betsie, whose household duties she has temporarily taken over:

Dearest Betsie,

I have washed fifteen pairs . . . let me say it again . . . *fifteen* pairs of gloves today. I had to gather every bit of my small amount of perseverance, and I did it this evening. As a result it feels as if my hands are glowing. Not all of them are thoroughly clean (the gloves that is) but they are washed. You enjoy that thought, don't you?

Poor Blackie is meowing. There is talk of getting rid of him because of some little accidents, and Mother does not want all the work that causes. In one word, I would find it *terrible*. I think that I am much too attached to him because I just don't want to think about his actually being sent away.

Monday morning: The question about Blackie has been solved! We have decided to keep him. Oh good!

It is encouraging to see how normal Corrie ten Boom was. She wanted to keep the cat, yet even at seventeen years old she was aware that she might be holding onto a personal desire too tightly. In later years she often said, "I must learn to hold earthly things lightly because if I do not the Lord might have to pry away my fingers, and that hurts."

Corrie with two cats, 1909   PHOTO COURTESY OF THE CORRIE TEN BOOM HOUSE FOUNDATION

"A New World Opened Up to Us"

Willem was the first child to leave home. In 1906 he went to study theology at the University of Leiden. Nollie took teachers' training and gained her diploma in 1909. Corrie studied at domestic science school, and she and Betsie were involved, with the aunts, in the household. The women of the Beje, like many Dutch, were scrupulous housekeepers.

In the old family letters to which I have access, there are no references to any other European countries during the time of the many comfortable and enriching advances mainly available to the European upper class of *La Belle Époque*. But in the rest of Europe "The Beautiful Time" also contained a strong military element. Nations were arming themselves, military parades were common and there was talk of unrest among Prussian princes.

The four young Ten Booms were often found at missionary conferences, where they would spend days learning from missionaries or overseas Christians. They studied other religions. When Corrie was in her late teens she, Willem, Betsie and Nollie got involved in a missions movement. Many years later, she recalled their first attendance at a missions conference:

> That first day I was so moved when the hundreds of people sang under the perfect guidance of an elderly missionary. Nollie was given the job of being a soloist for the first time in her life. The lectures were beautiful and deep, and in our spare time we talked things over in smaller groups. A new world opened up to us. . . .
>
> We had always been interested in missions, but now our horizons widened as real missionaries told their experiences.

The Ten Boom family members' bond was so strong that Mother once wrote, "We can hardly do without each other." They did not know the term "family values" or even talk about such a concept, but love, loyalty and commitment were clearly a normal reality for them.

The record shows, however, that community was as important to them as family. The Beje always welcomed anyone in Haarlem who was in need of advice, supper, prayer or fellowship with the Ten Booms. The whole family was deeply involved in the community, and as they grew up the children's involvement began to include the people of other countries.

And Afterward Receive Me

Eighteen-year-old Corrie wrote: "Today I had a quiet Sunday, not as pleasant as at home, but still Sunday. I went to church this morning and heard a fine sermon on an Old Testament text—that beautiful one from Psalm 73: 'Thou shalt guide me with thy counsel and afterward receive me to glory (KJV).'" In that letter she again refers to the good sermon and says that the singing was so beautiful that shivers ran down her spine.

Afterward You will receive me to glory. Even Corrie ten Boom, who had the most vivid imagination of anybody I have ever met, could not have envisaged her experiences in the 73 years that lay between that summer of 1910 and *Afterward*.

Although her country was able to remain neutral, it would not be long before World War I began. By the time it ended, 13 million lives would have been lost on both sides of the conflict. And that war would pave the way only 22 years later to another World War—for Corrie, "the deepest hell that man can create."

three

World War I

1912–1921

The Belle Époque, "The Beautiful Time," as the elite called it, was drawing to its close. From our vantage point in history, the sinking of the *Titanic* was the beginning of the end of the peace and prosperity that Europe had known for many decades.

Tuesday, April 15, 1912—Corrie's twentieth birthday—was also the date of the loss of the world's biggest ship, heralded as unsinkable, on its maiden voyage from England to America. The *Titanic* was fitted with the latest furnishings and contained electric elevators, several kitchens, libraries and even mechanical exercise machines shaped like camels and horses in the vast ship's gymnasium. Reports from survivors tell of passengers continuing to receive training on the mechanical animals even as the ship went down.

"When news of the disaster reached the Ten Boom household," described Corrie more than sixty years later, "Father went into the living room with Mother and called everybody who was at home to come together. We all had heard about the big ship—it was so safe, so luxurious. He was shocked by the news and could not take it in at first. I remember how he talked about it with us—and even with the customers.

"'Just imagine,' Father said, 'The passengers on the *Titanic* were not thinking much about danger. Those who belonged to the Lord Jesus were ready. Perhaps God called some at the last minute. The band played "Nearer My God to Thee" until the ship sank.'" Father ten Boom was implying perhaps that the music and words might have led many passengers to trust the Lord Jesus in the last moments of their lives.

The loss of 1,513 lives and the huge *Titanic* was a kind of precursor of the enormous destruction of people and property that Europe was about to face in the twentieth century.

A Time for War

After the establishment of the German empire in 1871, Germany quickly became an industrialized nation whose power challenged that of England, Russia and France. As Germany's wealth and power increased in the decades leading up to 1914, so did its people's glorification and military fortification of their fatherland. In response to this, other European lands began to arm themselves, spurred on by the ever-growing weapons industry. From 1910 onward, armies were mobilized and weapons arsenals were stockpiled in a way that Europe had never seen in peacetime.

Slowly two blocs came into being: Germany and Austria on one side and France and Russia, later joined by England, on the other. As 1914 approached, more than 25 million trained soldiers were at the ready on the European continent. Although there was no clear reason to declare war, it was as if the European powers wanted it. The Ten Boom family must have been deeply concerned about the rumors of war, but I have not found any trace of it in their frequent pre-war writings to each other.

Early in November 1913, nine months before World War I started, Willem moved out of the Beje. His studies had taken him away from home for years already, but this was a permanent move prompting his 21-year-old youngest sister, normally not a sentimental person, to write a letter in which we are given a glimpse of the love and admiration she had for him. Corrie wrote:

> The morning you left was wretched. It never occurred to me that we would all find it so difficult. Saying goodbye must have something to do with the "Fall." Perhaps this is very stupid of me because it is obvious, but please don't mind if I sound rather silly in this letter because ever since you left I have been wanting to write you a sentimental letter in which I tell you how much I love you, what a large place you fill in my life and perhaps thank you for I don't know what and that, of course, between a brother and sister would be too silly for words. I would be the first one to point out to somebody else how silly it would be to act in that way.
>
> Therefore, I think it would be better just to write and tell you that all the photographs came out well. Mother knows only about the two taken in the church. She will receive the others at [Christmas]. The large photograph of you is particularly good and full of life, perhaps a bit "great-manlike" but you are a "great man" in my eyes. I think my feelings are going in the wrong direction again and I had better close. Bye, Willem. Your Corrie.

Matters of health always featured strongly in the family's letters to each other, and this is evident in another letter from Corrie to Willem later that November, written while Father ten Boom was away for a few days:

> It was so nice that your letter came this particular day. I read it to Mother while she was still in bed. She could not sleep after Father left, but this afternoon she slept for a whole hour. Later in the afternoon I took her to Dr. van Veen, and his nurse took Mother's blood pressure. It was much too high. It

should have been 140, but hers was 210. The doctor took it very seriously and told her that if Mother did not do anything about it, she would have increasing problems with it, especially in about ten years' time.

Mother ten Boom was to die of a stroke eight years later.

Meanwhile, outside Holland's borders, the arms buildup continued. On June 28, 1914, the Austrian heir to the throne, Franz Ferdinand, was murdered in the Serbian capital of Sarajevo with his wife, Sophia. Germany rushed to the aid of Austria, which probably would have been capable of handling its own crisis, and World War I began in the first week of August.

Holland tried hard to stay neutral and succeeded. It was a small, militarily weak country living off the wealth of its large and rich colony of Indonesia. The Dutch could not possibly have defended the sea routes between Holland and Indonesia, and they certainly could not have defeated any state that might try to attack Indonesia. Germany was reluctant to occupy Holland because England would then have the excuse to take over the rich Dutch colony.

In a letter to Willem two months after the outbreak of war, Corrie refers to a military funeral:

Last week there was a funeral procession for the English officer who died here. The music played by the marine band was very beautiful and sadly impressive. Then the main band stopped playing and only a recorder sustained the tune, accompanied by some drummers on covered drums. That recorder was so beautiful and spooky. It was as if the sound came from another world, as in a fairy tale. Behind the carriage, on which lay the coffin covered with the English flag, was a large procession of soldiers and sailors, all walking very slowly. It was so strange to see these soldiers filing by step—step—step. The procession took half an hour to pass by. Perhaps it was because of all the artificial saddening things, or perhaps also because we knew that this was one of the thousand thousands, but we all felt unhappy inside.

This is the first reference to war. She was presumably referring to the many deaths taking place in the countries just outside Holland's borders. After initial advances, the war amounted to slow battling in the trenches, with resulting high loss of life on both sides.

Holland was an island of peace in the hell that most of Europe had become. In the first years of the war, industry, farming and shipping even made big profits. The British government oversaw the supply of food and other goods to Holland, with the proviso that these were not to be smuggled through to Germany for sale on the black market. But that happened to some extent. Between 1914 and 1917 the national income rose by almost fifty percent.

Less favorable conditions were to affect Holland soon, however, and the watch and clock business at the Beje would feel those effects. Writing to one of the girls' clubs that she and Corrie ran, Betsie gives us a picture of the family's circumstances in January 1916:

Dear children,

Please excuse me if my writing becomes incoherent. Nollie and Corrie are singing and playing the organ in the background, and I am finding it hard to concentrate. You have all been to our house, so you can probably picture me here in the living room. It is Sunday evening and the lamp is burning. Nollie is playing the organ near the window and all the family is upstairs reading. Everything looks Sunday-like in the house. I don't know why, but things look different from the way they do on weekdays.

As for my work, it is a strange time in business. I have never experienced anything like this in the fifteen years I have worked in the shop. At the moment we have enough clocks, but nobody, not even the cleverest economists, knows what the future will bring. However, if the war continues we will see some strange things. For example, for months not one clock came across the borders. Then a large wholesale Dutch dealer exported wagons full of chocolate. In exchange he received clocks. Watches are still coming through. Corrie needed a coat but could not find one. There were hardly any in a clothes shop where we have always had a lot of choice. In the end she bought a velvet one. You should see her—she looks so *chique*! She is worth a shilling more!

[Here Corrie adds a note:] I don't feel flattered at all. The shop assistant said, "You do need something chique," and Father said, "You really must take an elegant coat; you do need that."

A Time for Love

The Ten Boom family wholeheartedly supported Willem's decision to become a minister. As the only son and the sole university-trained member of the family, his career was followed with intense interest. He was ordained in the Dutch Reformed Church in April 1916. For the next month the Ten Booms lived at high-level mutual alert for Willem to be called to the pastorate of a church. They knew that it might come from the small village of Made in the beautiful southern province of Brabant, where a church had shown some interest in Willem. But the family knew that another candidate was also being considered.

When the decision to call Willem finally was made on May 16, the family's joy and cohesiveness was expressed in a letter written the next day from Corrie at the Beje to Betsie:

There is inexpressible happiness and gratitude in our hearts. Yesterday was a strange day. None of us wanted the other family members to know what we were thinking, but when the 1:15 p.m. post was expected we caught ourselves acting unusually. Nollie was sewing near the window from which she would be able to see the approach of the postman. Mother said goodbye to everybody on her way to her bed for an afternoon nap. Then I decided to shake out the mats in the passageway near the front door and found Mother sitting on the staircase. Both [of us] would have been near the letterbox through which the mailman might drop the good news. But the news did not come at 1:15 p.m. or at 4:00 p.m. . . .

When a telegram from Willem finally arrived, Corrie wrote, "Mother was jubilant! Tante Anna clapped her hands, and I threw my hat, coat and gloves in the air."

Now that Willem's call had come, plans could be made for his wedding. He was engaged to Christina (Tine, pronounced "Tina") van Veen, younger sister of the family doctor. The length of their engagement is unknown, but Dutch couples often had long engagements, probably due to the scarcity of suitable housing and work. Willem's wedding took place in the St. Bavo church on the market square near the Beje on August 23, 1916, when he was 29 and Tine was 32.

In a photograph of Tine and Willem seated in the Great Church at the end of the wedding ceremony, they are surrounded by about forty family members and friends—mainly unsmiling in the custom of the day. Corrie is in the top row of the photograph, standing near a handsome young man called Karel (not his real name). Karel and Willem became friends when they were theological students together. Corrie had first met him when she was fourteen and Karel had accompanied Willem to one of the Beje's many celebrations—perhaps a birthday party.

Corrie recalled later that from the moment she looked up into Karel's deep brown eyes, she fell irretrievably in love. Two years later, in 1908, while visiting Willem in his room at the University of Leiden, she met him again. He remembered her, and Corrie's hopes rose that a lasting friendship would develop that would lead to marriage. Now and then, through the years, Corrie and Karel came across each other at various family events.

In *The Hiding Place*, Corrie allowed her co-writers John and Elizabeth Sherrill to tell the story of Karel. They deal sensitively and respectfully with a subject to which Tante Corrie made no reference during the time I was with her, except once near the end of her life.

Another Route for Love to Travel

Shortly after Willem and Tine's wedding, Corrie and her family and many friends went to the village of Made to hear Willem's first sermon as pastor. A first sermon was always a momentous occasion in the Dutch Reformed Church. Corrie had looked forward to the occasion with extra excitement because she knew Karel would be there.

Indeed he was, and during the days they spent in Made, he showed much interest in Corrie. They took many walks together and even talked about the future. Although the word "marriage" was not mentioned, Corrie was led to believe that Karel had a serious intent toward her—until Willem explained that his parents, who had sacrificed much for his theological education, were determined that Karel should marry into a wealthy family. Corrie protested that his parents' wishes did not necessarily represent what Karel wanted. Her brother's response must have dealt the biggest blow Corrie had yet received in her 24 years. She describes it in *The Hiding Place:*

> Willem fixed his sober, deep-set eyes on mine. "He will do it, Corrie. I don't say he wants it. To him it is just a fact of life like any other. When we would talk about girls we liked—at the university—he would always say at the end, 'Of course I could never marry her. It would kill my mother.'"[1]

Willem's prediction soon proved true. Karel announced his engagement to the daughter of wealthy members of the church where he was assistant pastor. It was Father ten Boom who comforted a grieving Corrie that fall of 1916.

"Corrie," he told her when they were alone, "do you know what hurts so very much? It's love. Love is the strongest force in the world, and when it is blocked that means pain. There are two things we can do when this happens. We can kill the love so that it stops hurting. But then, of course, part of us dies, too. Or, Corrie, we can ask God to open up another route for that love to travel."[2]

That hour Corrie gave up her feelings for Karel: "Lord, I give to You the way I feel about Karel, my thoughts about our future—oh, You know! Everything! Give me your way of seeing Karel instead. Help me to love him that way. That much."[3]

Although without doubt Corrie had the same deep emotional longings of most women, it was not long before she realized that there never would be another Karel and that her life would be spent as a single woman.

Perhaps the contents have nothing to do with Karel or her future, but in an undated letter to her mother written at approximately the time of her prayer of relinquishment of marriage, the normally effervescent and humorous Corrie displays a vulnerable side. She had just attended a mission conference:

> I must tell you about a wonderfully treasured moment at the conference. We women were lying in bed in the dormitory. We shared difficulties and comforted each other. And then all became quiet . . . even in the noisy rooms around us. We were dozing, and all of a sudden we heard very softly from far away, yet quite distinctly, the "Ave Maria" being played on a flute, and oh, you don't know what a lonely sound that is, a flute in an open field. It gripped me so much that I sat on the windowsill crying softly.

She never spoke to me about Karel except with joy in 1978 when, during the reading of a newly published Dutch book about the Second World War, she told me that Karel had been among the Dutch Reformed ministers who had not gone along with the edicts of the Nazis. "I have often wondered about that," she told me. When, in her eighties, Corrie learned of Karel's death in the Netherlands, she wrote a note of sympathy to his widow. This was the last I know of Tante Corrie's thoughts about the man she once had loved.

Life During the War

In 1917, the third year of the war, rations were cut and the Dutch, especially the laborers, suffered hunger and cold from then until the end of the war. In June of that year Mother wrote to Willem and Tine in Made that she had been able to buy a basketful of purslane (an edible weed) for a couple of guilders and that Corrie made eight bottles of preserves from it. She asked Tine if she had any potatoes. At the Beje they were able to purchase a few kilos quite frequently.

Corrie's zest for living is indicated in a letter dated May 1917 from Betsie to the family, although we do not know what caused Betsie's merriment: "My handkerchief was wet through with tears of laughter when I read Corrie's postcard. I could not even read it aloud to Tante Jans."

At about the same time, in another letter, Corrie expressed her love for travel: "I will be going to Leiden tomorrow on an errand for Tante Jans. Lovely! Whenever there is an opportunity to celebrate or to travel, I am happy!"

On July 8, 1917, while Betsie was in Made awaiting with Willem and Tine the birth of their first child, Corrie wrote to tell her, "This week I gave a private demonstration of the cooking bag and the newspaper case for a family. We made the cooking case from a suitcase and it held three large pans. It was a success."

Sixty years later, when I was living with her in Placentia, California, Tante Corrie explained this strange activity to me. She volunteered to cook supper for guests one evening and told me she wanted to use a cooking method she had learned during World War I. It involved partially cooking the food, wrapping each item very thoroughly in newspaper and then placing the items in a cooking case all packed together with the lid closed. The idea was that the food in its tightly enclosed wrappings would continue to cook slowly. Less fuel was used, of course—a good and economical wartime method! That night a truly excited Tante Corrie presented her meal which, after having sat in newspaper wrapping for several hours, could not be described as tasty. Although he thanked her profusely, one of the guests said to me privately, "That was terrible."

We can tell from that same letter to Betsie in early July 1917 that Corrie was not particularly fond of housework. She addresses it while referring to her course at Bible school in Haarlem:

Earlier this week I had some exams. As you know, I had excellent opportunity to get ready. The day before the exam I got up at 5:00 a.m. There were two boxes of trash that I dragged from the cellar to the street with great difficulty. Then I made Nollie's sandwich for her lunch and cleaned the living room. When the trash man came he did not want to take the rubbish with him. I pulled it into the house again and had to sweep the passage, the staircase and the street. By 8:00 p.m. I had not studied one letter.

Corrie goes on to tell Betsie that she thought the exam went well and wrote, "I am glad about that, for there is nothing more discouraging than bad papers and looking after the housekeeping with no help."

Although the terrible war continued to cost the lives of hundreds of thousands of Europeans outside the Dutch island of neutral safety, life went on for the Ten Booms. Named after his grandfather, Tine and Willem's expected baby, "Little Cas," arrived on July 13, 1917. The next week, on July 22, Father Casper wrote to Willem, Tine and Betsie, telling of his longing to come to them and explaining why at the moment it was not possible.

I am fairly well and do have some income, but I have such an excessive amount to pay in bills that I am in straightened circumstances. Bills seem to be coming from all sides. Yet I have nothing to complain about and no doubt I will be helped through. . . .

We greatly long to see that child, our little grandchild, and hold him in our arms. But it seems the time for this has not yet come, otherwise the Lord would have given me some more money. . . . May the Lord bless you and the little one and may He enable us to send something, though it is not possible yet.

He must have received a quick answer to prayer because four days later Mother Cor sent twenty guilders to Betsie: "Ten guilders are for you so that you can give a guilder to the nurse and pay your travel costs with the rest. The other ten guilders are for the cradle and other expenses for little Cas."

From correspondence in early August we learn that the Dutch government had to restrict the use of gas. Betsie and Corrie were away from home at a conference, and a letter from their mother offered the mysterious advice: "Corrie, you must not stay away too long for, oh child, I fear it will all be too much for you. Don't use too much *zieleleven* (soul-life, spiritual life) for that is as bad as using too much gas. Betsie, please look after her. Keep each other calm."

A P.S. from Tante Anna indicates that the Beje household missed Corrie's power of organization: "Corrie, cubic meters of gas are being burned! I tremble to see your face when you come home! I keep reminding Father to watch his meter usage continually. You must come home soon again in order to keep us close to being economical."

Two days later Mother wrote about the arrival of electricity at the Beje, paid for by Tante Jans: "We do like the electric light, but oh dear, Mr. Koen said that gas light was really cheaper, and now Tante Jans is very crestfallen."

In mid-August Nollie, a trained schoolteacher, left the Beje to take a teaching position in Amsterdam. Sufficient housing has been a problem in Holland to this day, so there was no question of her finding even so much as an apartment. She was able to rent rooms in a large house. She and the family were impressed with this very independent move.

In November 1917, Corrie wrote to Betsie, again referring to the fuel situation:

> Now that we have to use fuel so economically we often eat upstairs, which makes the living room a terrible mess. The table becomes a dresser and the side window a steam funnel to take away the smells of cooking meat and cabbage.
>
> This week I wanted to put everything aside in order to prepare for the big examination in dogmatics, which awaits me tomorrow. It is filling my thoughts day and night. In every free moment I am trying to learn a sentence, and my dreams are filled with talks on original sin, the unity of the human race, evolution theory and Pelagianism.

Corrie's Bible Education

During this time Corrie was growing strongly in her knowledge of her faith. In 1910, when she first took courses at the Bible school, Corrie had written to Willem: "There are so many problems assailing me at this time that I cannot handle them. The interpretation of the liberal pastors sometimes gets me very confused. If I did not have Father, I would never manage."

Several years later, during the war, she sent another letter to Willem that is evidence of her level of spiritual growth:

> I feel there are plenty of dangers around us. They cause us to look for reality, for a living faith, some solid point in this ocean of influences. We keep hearing about Christian moral consciousness, denial of man's corrupt nature and glorifying

of man's intellect. In this atmosphere, many ministers are losing ground.

Maybe I am exaggerating a little, but I feel a little out of balance myself. I do not belong in our Reformed Church, nor in the Christian Reformed Church. . . . Also, the other smaller fundamentalist circles do not satisfy me. I have studied too much church history for that. But then, where do I belong?

In a letter to Nollie in December 1917, Corrie describes the beauty of her previous day's outing at yet another conference while expressing her early love for theology and teaching:

What Christmas-like scenes we saw! At 4:00 p.m. the moon was already shining brightly, and its reflection on the white snow made it as clear as midday. We went to the Wilhelmina dune, and the view from there over the snowy dunes and the white roofs in the clear moonlight and the lights of Haarlem . . . it was so unreal and so like a fairy story that I would not have been surprised if I had met dwarves or nymphs.

Pastor Creutzberg gave a beautiful sermon. It was so stalwart and Calvinistic, and he had such beautiful diction! The whole church, full to overflowing, hung on his every word. He set our thoughts in motion in such a way that when I went to bed I quickly wrote part of my sermon. The consequence of this was that I got to sleep very late and preached the rest of the night. Don't be afraid that I shall ever deliver that sermon, at least not in the near future. But it is a very good exercise to write down one's thoughts. You then become aware that your subconscious is a store of thoughts, and that while you are writing, the sentences and ideas come all on their own.

On January 20, 1918, Betsie wrote a letter to Corrie, who was shortly to receive her Bible school diploma. Apart from discussing household affairs, ration coupons and the availability of bread, Betsie tells about a visit from Nollie, who had now been living in her own rooms in Amsterdam for about six months:

Tonight again we had a long discussion about feminism, especially Father and Nollie. That funny child has only just started thinking of these matters now that she has left home. Funny, isn't it? She is greatly enjoying Father's counsel and conversations. I am also in the middle of feminism affairs because I am reading Naber's book about our aunts and great-aunts. It deals especially with the forerunners of feminism.

Child, how easy things are for us. Without realizing it, we are reaping the fruits of their troubles. Fifty years ago you would not have dared to think of studying, as you are doing now. Girls had to wash the dishes and embroider and marry. And it never entered their minds to live like Nollie, having rooms of her own and earning her living. You really should read the book.

The Ten Boom sisters could never have foreseen the work that Corrie would later undertake as a single woman, especially that of speaking. In her early twenties, she enjoyed singing at gospel meetings but was not yet convinced that it was proper for a woman to preach. This was an important issue in the Church at the time, and she wrote Willem about her feelings on the matter:

Pastor B. sent me a request to preach on December 12. I discussed it with Father and, following his advice, I declined the invitation.

In the evangelism course I took we did not agree on the question of whether the women of our present day may preach or not. Father says it will cause me to lose my femininity; I am 75 percent in agreement with him but would like to have your opinion on this.

This urge to evangelize—to tell people the glorious message of the Gospel—gives me a deep longing to speak out loud, as loudly as I can. But as far as that is concerned, I am afraid there is some vanity connected with it.

There is no record of Willem's response, but Corrie obviously eventually changed her mind about the propriety of a woman teaching the Gospel! See appendix 2 for her views on the subject in 1960.

The End of the Great War

In 1917 the United States came to the aid of the French and the British. The Germans had lost ground and on November 10, 1918, the German kaiser fled to the Dutch border for refuge from the revolution in his own country. The official end of the First World War took place at 11:00 a.m. on November 11, 1918. The Allies had lost five million men in the previous four years and three months, and on the German-Austrian side three million had died.

On November 11, President Woodrow Wilson announced to the American people: "The armistice was signed this morning. Everything for which America fought has been accomplished. It will now be our fortunate duty to assist by example, by sober, friendly counsel and by material aid in the establishment of just democracy throughout the world." On that same day, however, a news release told of the German foreign secretary's "earnest" appeal to President Wilson "to mitigate the fearful conditions" of the Versailles agreement, which "the German government had to accept."

Mother Cor's Strokes and Death

At the end of 1918, Mother Cor, who a few years earlier had experienced a mild stroke, suffered a major one. Corrie, busy with housework in another part of the Beje, decided to check on her mother. Running into the kitchen, she found Cor at the sink with the water running out of the basin and onto the floor. Her mother was "staring strangely," Corrie said later, and could say just one word: "Corrie." Assisting her mother to bed, Corrie called for the other members of the household and dispatched the shop apprentice to fetch Dr. van Veen. At first it seemed that Mother would not live, but after two months of serious illness and semi-consciousness, she opened her eyes and looked around her. Though she suffered initial paralysis, she regained the use of her arms and legs and was even able to be present at Nollie's wedding on July 23, 1919. But she never spoke again. Communication was possible through a little game, something like Twenty Questions:

"What is it, Mama? You're thinking of someone!"

"Yes."

"Someone in the family?"

"No."

"A woman?"

"Yes."

Mother passed away in 1921. Nearly six decades later, Tante Corrie and I were standing at the sink in her bathroom. The previous year she had suffered a stroke that had taken her powers of speech, but she had made a fairly good recovery from initial paralysis. On this morning of her second and major stroke, I was assisting her in getting ready for the day. As I helped her find the sleeves of the jacket to her dress, Tante Corrie looked at me strangely and began to lean to the right. I took hold of her and led her to her bed. She lost all the strength regained on her right side and was in a partially conscious state. It seemed she could not live. But one day after several weeks of serious illness, as suddenly as she had lost consciousness, she woke up and looked around. Although she regained strength and lived for four more years, her speech never returned. We worked out a system of communication very similar to the one she had used with her mother decades before.

"Tante Corrie, are you thinking about a person?" (The Ten Booms were usually thinking of people other than themselves.)

"Yes."

"A man?"

"No."

"Does she live in the United States?"

We were to play the Twenty Questions guessing game for nearly five years.

four

The Years between
the World Wars

1921–1939

In her later years Corrie was fond of saying, "Every experience God gives us, every person He puts in our lives is the perfect preparation for the future that only He can see." During the two world wars God brought many experiences and many people into the lives of the Ten Booms. Between the wars Corrie and Betsie worked with young women and became foster parents of many children. And the letters during this time help us to know Betsie better.

Father Casper

"This is the saddest day of my life," said Father when his wife passed away in October 1921. "Thank you, Lord, for giving her to me."

For me, these words sum up the attitude and living faith of the Ten Boom family. In the deepest grief he had yet known, Casper simply stated that fact, and then turned to the Lord with a thankful heart that his deeply loved Cor had been given to him for 37 years. Years later, telling about that day and the months that followed, Corrie said that her father displayed no self-pity. He knew where his wife was, and he knew that life and the Lord's work had to go on.

In Corrie's writing and speaking of Casper, we see a resolute, not-in-a-hurry kind of Christian leader. His matter-of-fact Dutchness was part of that, but this watchmaker's stability was based on an active and daily living faith that "all our times are in God's hands, even the difficult ones." Theologians call this the sovereignty of God, which, simply said, means that He who is all-loving and always good determines the paths His children take, allowing pain and suffering to come to them for an eventually good purpose. Casper ten Boom lived his life from that perspective. So did his daughter Corrie. It was the basis for all her witness and work and is the main life lesson of this book.

Tante Corrie's Greatest Lesson

I am often asked to tell the greatest lesson I learned during my seven years with Tante Corrie. The answer is "a high view of the sovereignty of God." But I do not usually say those words because through overuse they have lost their real meaning for some, and for new Christians in our generation they can sound a bit pompous and not very practical. But the truth is that I can describe just about any lesson I learned from her and it will come back every time to: "All my times are in His hands."

From Corrie I learned, for example, how to deal with my tendency toward self-pity. During the months we traveled together my tasks as her companion included things like travel arrangements, stage arrangements, diet needs and crowd control—all in fast-moving repetition as we journeyed from city to city. I was busier than I had ever been, and my tendency to feel sorry for myself was encouraged by the way I was treated sometimes by those who invited Corrie to speak. One such difficult occasion took place in a flat, northern city in the United States when her host, a minister, seeing that I was Corrie's servant, began to treat me in a cold and distant manner—as though I were his servant, too. I found this most unfair. I had enough to do already. Why was this unpleasant man making life more complicated?

Tante Corrie was aware that I was feeling off-balance about this, but she did not really understand the effect the minister's behavior was having on me. This does not mean that she was uncaring. She was just resolutely doing her job as speaker and counselor. In her mid-eighties she could have been forgiven if she had complained about fatigue and inconvenience, but I never saw in her any hint of self-pity in all the time we were together.

On this and another occasion, she took me to task quite firmly about self-pity, calling it a particularly destructive sin. She helped me see that even the most difficult things in our lives cannot occur unless the Lord allows them. "It is not so much what happens, but how we take it that is important," she taught me. "All our times are in God's hands, even the difficult ones." I can see now that while the minister's treatment of me was wrong, so was my reaction. A "poor-me" attitude blinds us to God's larger purposes. After her imprisonment Corrie prayed that God would help her see her sufferings "a little bit" from His point of view. He answered that prayer. He showed her that her sufferings could be used in a far-reaching, redemptive way in the lives of others.

Children Join the Household

As soon as the war ended, the Ten Booms looked for ways to help German children. Many of them were suffering from severe malnutrition as a result of their country's defeat. Always happy when making plans, the sisters discussed the possibility of bringing some of the children to Holland, providing them with good food and loving care and sending them back to their country healthy. Father had many contacts among the watchmakers of Holland, and he wrote letters to them asking if they could provide temporary homes for German children. Many responded, and arrangements were made for the children to arrive by train on a certain day to be met by their prospective host families. Father, Betsie and Corrie went to Haarlem's railway station to see that each child went with the proper family.

One shy, thin girl of about ten had not been assigned to a family. "We'll take her home with us," said Father. And the host family of eight-year-old Willy, who lived on the streets of Berlin, was not at the station to meet him. Father discovered that because of illness at their house, the family was unable to take Willy. He, too, was taken home to the Beje. These were the first of many children who went to live there during the post–World War I years.

A Change at the Beje

In the early 1920s, after the German children returned home, a change occurred in the division of labor in the Beje. Of the three aunts, only Tante Anna was still living. All the years the children were growing up and during the final illnesses of her sisters, she had worked hard at housekeeping. Now her own health was failing.

Betsie had long been her father's helper in the watch shop, although she and Corrie did change tasks now and then. Corrie's main job had always been in the household assisting Tante Anna. Although as a younger woman she had not shown a particular liking for housekeeping, Corrie grew to find the work "challenging and creative."

When Betsie became ill during a flu epidemic, Corrie had to take her place in the watch shop, where she had previously spent little time. "I felt as if I had two left hands," she said, recalling those early days. "It was a different world—meeting people, remembering their particular likes and dislikes, seeing in facts and figures the precarious balance of the family business."

After Betsie recovered, Corrie made a suggestion: "Why don't we exchange jobs for a few months, so I can learn more about shopkeeping? I am so terribly ignorant of what goes on in the business." Her sister agreed. As the months passed, both sisters were happy with the arrangement. Betsie had a particular flair for beauty and order, and this was reflected in rearranged cupboards, flowers on the table and new variety at mealtimes. The new working arrangement became permanent.

Holland's First Woman Watchmaker

Corrie settled into her new work with characteristic enthusiasm. She saw ways to improve the business, such as asking Father why he closed the windows of the watch shop in the evenings when far more people walked through the Barteljorisstraat at that time than during the day. Realizing that the stock of watches and clocks was insufficient, she purchased more and soon had a larger inventory than the watch shop had ever known. That side of the business was soon left in her hands.

After a while, Corrie realized how useful it would be if she were able to help not only by running the shop but also in actual watch repairing. She asked her father if he would teach her the trade. Immediately Father agreed, telling her that he would like to send her to Switzerland for training and that she could well become a better watchmaker than he was.

"He had a great trust in my abilities," she said. Corrie inherited this trait from him—trust in the abilities of others. She was able to make a person feel he were the only person in the world who could fulfill a particular task.

Through the sale of an expensive watch, Father was able to send Corrie to Switzerland to learn watchmaking by serving apprenticeships in two factories. She gained her certificate in 1924 at the age of 32 and became, as she liked to tell, "Holland's first licensed woman watchmaker."

The Foster Children

After Tante Anna's death in 1925, only Father, Betsie and Corrie were left in the Beje. The same year, a new way of life came to the old house with the arrival of foster children. Many Dutch missionaries worked in Holland's large colony of Indonesia, and their children completed elementary and some high school grades in that country. But when the time came for further education they were sent to the Netherlands. Many of the children did not have relatives or friends with whom they could stay. Having visited the large institution-like housing where many of them stayed, Corrie and Betsie felt sorry for the children who were paying such a high price of separation and loneliness. When Willem, therefore, came to the Beje one day with a special request, they quickly responded, and after saying, "Let's pray about it first," Father did, too.

Willem, a member of the boards of several mission societies for Indonesia, had just heard about three missionary children who urgently needed somewhere to stay in Holland. Before long, Betsie (40), Corrie (33) and Father (65) became the foster parents of two girls and a boy: Puck (14), Hans (12) and their brother Hardy (15).

Betsie and Corrie shared their new responsibilities. Betsie took care of food and clothing, and Corrie, who reckoned her tasks were more fun, was responsible for sports and music.

The Generosity of the Ten Booms

There was never much money at the Beje. Most Dutch families had to economize as much as possible. Many were out of work in the years between the wars, and there was much poverty. This meant there were fewer clients in the watch shop. Most people did not have the means to buy items such as clocks and watches.

In spite of this, the Ten Booms' generosity to needy children increased. More children joined the household, including two girls named Lessie and Miep. At one point the Beje was home for seven children. "I never had so much fun as in those years when the foster children were with us in the Beje," said Corrie, recalling memories later in life. But it must be noted that Corrie frequently used that expression. She lived firmly in the present with an eye to the future. I heard her say "I have never had such fun" countless times, and I am sure she was right in each case!

More than fifty years after she came to live at the Beje, Hans, one of the first foster girls, described life there in a letter:

> Life with the Ten Booms was simple but a lot of fun. They understood the art of enjoying every small thing. I remember especially that Tante Corrie and Tante Betsie both enjoyed life intensely because they believed that everything that was given to them was a gift from God. But they did not over-spiritualize.
>
> Tante Corrie was a very gifted person. She would say about her gifts: "Those are things a person cannot make for herself. You must, therefore, thank God for the gifts you have been given."

Hans went on to tell about Father's attitude in a house that was always busy not just with the foster children but with the friends whom they often brought home:

> Opa (Grandfather), as we young ones called him, was never bothered by all the noise going on around him. He just kept working quietly. He always saw good in us. "They are wonderful children," he used to say. "They never quarrel."
>
> In those years at the Beje I grew from a girl to a young woman. I thank God even now that he gave me these substitute parents while my own father and mother were missionaries in

Indonesia. It was a privilege to spend those important years with the Ten Boom family.

Of course it was actually not always the case that the children never quarreled. As in all normal households they needed discipline now and then, and Corrie applied it. Father, however, was never aware of disharmony.

It might seem that Corrie was busy enough in the watch shop business and in caring for the foster children. But she also gave Bible lessons in schools and held classes and a special church service on Sunday afternoons for mentally disabled children, for whom she had particular respect and love.

The Clubs

And there was to be much more work. In keeping with her family's enthusiasm for learning of the needs of others, she found herself one day at a meeting of the Association of Women Friends of the Young Girl. She heard a speaker talk passionately about the help and guidance needed by girls aged thirteen to eighteen. Sunday school classes ended when a child reached the age of twelve or thirteen, and the YWCA (Young Women's Christian Association) provided group meetings only for girls of eighteen and above.

Betsie and Corrie talked about the need for structured Christian activities for the young girls who in their early teens would be faced with decisions that would affect their whole lives. They began making plans.

Betsie, who had taught Sunday school at the St. Bavo, the Great Church, for many years, obtained lists of her former pupils. Invitations to be part of a new club were issued, and teenage girls responded. The name of the first club was the Church Walk Club. Corrie and Betsie met the girls on one of Haarlem's bridges each Sunday at 8:30 a.m. They took a long walk together to the dunes, where they played games and talked before walking back to the 10:00 a.m. service at church. The club grew in number and soon began to meet on Wednesdays, too, for an evening of games and a short Bible story with a practical application.

From this small beginning many other clubs were formed. It was soon necessary for Betsie and Corrie to find and train more leaders. Both were strong motivators—"even Betsie in her quiet way," said Corrie—and it was not long before an enthusiastic group of able young women began to get together every week to discuss activities for the next club meetings. They learned games from each other to play with the girls, and Corrie taught them how to give a Bible message with a short story so that each leader knew how to do it in her own club. Soon, more and more girls showed the desire to be part of these clubs, officially known as Haarlem's Girls' Clubs. Their purpose was to teach the girls the Gospel and keep them off the streets. During weekly meetings of the club leaders, everybody took a turn telling a story from the Bible while the rest critiqued. The types of questions asked were:

Was the Gospel clear?

How was her first sentence? Did it attract attention?

Was there humor?

What help was offered for the girls this week?

What importance did the story have for eternity?

Did she describe colors, movements?

Did she draw clear pictures with good illustrations?

Was it an inspiration for action, for faith, for endurance?

This training was invaluable not just for the girls but for Corrie herself. In thousands of talks across the world in 64 countries she applied the speaking principles she taught her club leaders in the 1920s and 1930s. When I was with her in the mid-1970s, she still took each speaking appointment very seriously, preparing arduously for each talk. Sometimes we went over her talks together. My respect rose when she, who had given basically the same message countless times, asked me to be sure to tell her if there was anything she had left out.

In the 1920s so many enthusiastic members joined the clubs that the garden and park areas where they had been meeting were no longer suitable. Premises were rented.

There was a club for every activity in which the girls showed interest: music, singing, folk dancing, English, sewing, embroidery, gymnastics, and so on. Eventually Corrie was to start a mixed club, almost unheard of at the time, where boys and girls could get to know each other in a natural setting. Halfway through the evening, the club leader gathered the girls together and read a short piece from the Bible, after which they had long discussions.

Once each year the clubs came together for a performance in Haarlem's concert hall, where nearly every club had the opportunity to demonstrate its abilities. The performance started with all 250 to 300 girls marching onto the platform. They then sang a song, and Corrie gave a five-minute talk to the approximately one thousand people in attendance. One year her subject was "God's Telephone Number Is Never Busy," and another year, "Have You Tuned Your Radio to the Right Station?"

The young men of the mixed Friends' Club provided musical accompaniment for the whole evening. Describing the first performance, Corrie later wrote:

> They were nervous about playing, and I wanted to boost their confidence. I took a violin in my left hand and the bow in my right hand. Then I turned the bow over so that it could not touch the violin's strings and acted as if I were a real musician. I don't know how many people in the concert hall saw my antics. There was no music coming from my violin, but we had lots of fun. And I needed to help the boys only that one time.[1]

Under Corrie's leadership, a Christian Girl Scout movement, the Triangle Girls, grew out of the Haarlem's Girls' Clubs. Many girls became part of the movement, including some with physical handicaps. As the club work grew, Corrie began to hold summer camps for the girls. At first they used tents, then later a building that had room for about sixty girls.

Decades later, Kitty, one of the club girls, wrote about her experiences:

> I came to know Tante Corrie when I was fourteen. I first met her in the Haarlem Girls' Club where I took the catechism class. After that, I was confirmed in the St. Bavo. In those days nearly all the club girls belonged to the working class. Our families had little money. There was a lot of unemployment. But because of the Girls' Clubs I was able to attend several camps and even went on a journey along the Rhine River.
>
> At the camps we had a campfire each evening and we always paid good attention to what Tante Corrie said in her talks. Her simple way of telling things made a deep impression on me and many others. And she always gave us something to think about after the talk ended. I always listened closely, looking at her beautiful, friendly eyes, which spoke so much love to us. Tante Corrie was a wonderful pedagogue. And she had such a great sense of humor that I can hardly describe it. She laid in my heart the basis of faith.

The Rise of Anti-Semitism

Willem ten Boom, after working in village pastorates—first in Made and then in Zuijlen—began to be increasingly concerned at the rise of anti-Semitism in Europe. He spent much of his spare time studying the subject at the University of Utrecht.

He said to Tine, "I was captivated by the subject of anti-Semitism from the start, but now that I am really getting into it, it is taking possession of me. I can no longer get away from it. The Jewish question is haunting me. It is so dangerous. Anti-Semitism has repercussions that will affect the whole world." Leaving the pastorate in 1926, he began working for the Society for Israel, and this led to doctoral studies at the University of Leipzig in Germany. The title of his thesis was "The Birth of Modern Racial Anti-Semitism in France and Germany."

From Leipzig he wrote to Tine, who was home with their four children: "I expect that in a few years' time there will be worse pogroms than ever before. Countless Jews from the east will come across the border to seek refuge in our country. We must prepare for that situation."

Betsie

It would not be long before the gathering clouds of war would darken and Betsie would lose her life. She and Corrie shared a deep sisterly love, respect and closeness. They enjoyed being co-workers, co-conspirators and co-planners for the good of thousands in their home city—those in their Bible classes, Girl Scout and club members, their foster children, neighbors and friends, many of whom visited the Beje. Photographs, writings and stories from this time show us what Corrie was like—a strong, extroverted leader and an unconditional lover of people with a huge sense of humor and an infectious faith.

But what was Betsie like? In the few photographs we have of her she allows no smile and even looks a bit formidable. I think Corrie wanted us to know Betsie better because in her mideighties, when we were living in California, she sent letters to friends, relatives and previous club girls and foster children asking them to send her their written remembrances of Betsie. She wanted to write a book about her sister. Her stroke in 1978 prevented that desire from materializing, but I often thought about the slim, cream-colored file hanging in its green casing in the left-hand drawer of her desk with the tag "Book, Betsie" in her handwriting. And I felt regret that Corrie's version of Betsie's life would never be told.

She had written notes, however, that were intended for her proposed book, and she had kept several letters about Betsie.

These give us insight into some of the lessons Corrie wanted us to learn from Betsie's life. She starts with a reference to foster child Lessie:

> Several years of Betsie's and my life were occupied with our foster children. When the girls were all in their crowded bedrooms at night, Betsie, Father and I came together and talked over what had happened during the day. Then we prayed and committed all of them to the care of the heavenly Father whom we knew loved them and from whom we expected the wisdom and love we needed to guide these teenagers. . . .
>
> I do not remember ever to have laughed so much as in that time. Once Betsie said, "I told Lessie today to give a spring cleaning to the kitchen cupboard. She did it with much joy, singing the whole time, but boy, how impractical she is! Girls who grow up in Indonesia do not learn housekeeping because their parents have servants who do that work. But as for my girls here, I will teach them housekeeping."
>
> "How will you find time for it?" I asked her. "They all are studying to be teachers."
>
> "Yes, and the day they finish they will find a job and leave the care of their Aunt Betsie. But I have found a solution. I have written to their parents about my plan. I told them: 'There is a great chance that your daughter will marry in the future. I can congratulate the young man who will bring Puck to the altar and is willing to stay with her for better and for worse. I know that as soon as she has her teaching diploma she will get a job. How can I teach her the noble art of cooking and housekeeping when she is so busy at the moment with her studies and later with her job? What about giving me permission to keep her at home for a year before she goes to the last class at college?'
>
> "I also have written about my plans to the mission board and wonder what they will think of my revolutionary thoughts."
>
> I remember how in the following days Betsie received enthusiastic letters one after the other from the parents and mission boards. So Betsie took the girls away from school one at a time, and she taught all of them how to cook, clean and

organize the big household. We also found we could finally
enjoy the music, sport and other hobbies for which we had
not had enough time when they were studying. And most of
the girls helped me at the Clubs, first as Club girls and later
as assistants.

How did it work out? Later when I went to the house of
one of the married girls, I remember that the kitchen, closets
and rooms all were arranged in the same way as in our house.
Hans' daughters told me that when there was an argument
about a household decision their mother said, "Tante Betsie
said . . ." and that convinced them. Certainly the menus were
like Betsie's—Betsie's soup, Betsie's puddings. Betsie's spirit
was alive in that home. She had the art of making everyday
life important and joyful."

What did Betsie look like, and how did her voice sound? In a
letter written six decades later, a woman named Jo who as a child
visited the Beje one afternoon in 1911 gave her perception of the
difference between Corrie and Betsie: "Betsie had a soft speaking voice, which suited her angelic and fragile being. She kept
working at the housekeeping very quietly—a very caring woman.
It seemed to me that Tante Corrie was the strong one, someone
everybody could depend upon whenever that was necessary."

Previous club girl Henk van Langelaar described, "Once I was
at the Beje for a meal. Tante Betsie reminded me of fine china."
And a family friend said, "She always reminded me of a cameo
brooch." Another foster child recalled: "I remember Betsie as a
'Martha' figure, an always-serving Christian."

A relative wrote:

You asked me to tell you my memories of Tante Betsie. The
thing I remember most is the connection she maintained
with the family ancestors through old letters, daguerrotypes
and old pictures, which she lovingly colored and framed. The
past lived for Betsie (in contrast with her brother and sisters
who much more—sometimes exclusively it seemed—looked

toward the future). How Betsie enjoyed books like David Copperfield and those by Louisa May Alcott! She loved, understood and knew about antiques, and especially art. She transferred her love for paintings to me during the various visits I made with her to the Frans Hals Museum. At first I went with her reluctantly to do her a favor, but her enthusiastic descriptions of the pictures won me over and I developed a permanent interest in art. I also remember her scrapbooks in which she glued colorful advertisements for recipes and foreign newspaper clippings.

Sometimes she received letters from Indonesia from the parents of the Beje foster children in which they requested that she buy and send them certain items that could not be found in Indonesia. Those were not always easy errands. She once told me she had to go to many shops before she found the desired article. Nothing was ever too much for her. I remember that she was always cheerful and very neatly dressed

Hans Kapner, whose home I just described and whom I mentioned earlier as one of the first foster children to come to the Beje, wrote:

The first thing I want to say about Tante Betsie is that she was *there*. She was always *there*. She was a balanced, quiet woman who was involved in every part of the life of the Beje. You could really say that she had a central place in the Beje. She never sought the limelight, but if for some reason she had to give the lead, she stepped forward with controlled grace.

Betsie was the only member of the family who could not sing and who did not play an instrument. Even so, she was very musical and enjoyed good music intensely. She was able to determine musical nuances and to direct our attention to them.

She was definitely before her time in the way she used language. I always noticed this trait, for instance, when Grandfather and Tante Corrie were not there and Betsie prayed at the table. The first time I heard her address God without using "Thou" or "Thine" I felt a bit shocked, as she just called Him "You" in the modern way. But later I thought, "Yes, that is how it should be. That is how we speak to each other, that is how you talk to your friend; so why not talk to your great Friend in such a way?" That helped me a lot later when I was a teacher. It meant much more to the children if I did not use old-fashioned terms in prayer.

I think Betsie was a very intelligent woman. When we arrived at the Beje as foster children, she was auditing a class in Hebrew in the top [last] class of high school. She used the Hebrew often at home, following Grandfather's Bible reading in her Hebrew Bible. Sometimes she would say, "I thought that this is the way it should be translated." And when Grandfather or Tante Corrie had to give a talk somewhere, it was often Betsie who suggested a subject or came up with the idea on which the speech would be based.

She was always happy when I came to the kitchen to study while she cooked. She liked me to study aloud and often commented, "Oh, how interesting." She was particularly interested in history.

She had a great need of *gezelligheid*, both for herself and for others. She showed this in all kinds of small ways in ordinary daily life. On Sunday afternoons, for example, we always drank tea upstairs in the parlor. She laid a large tray with a matching mat and took the best cups from the cupboard and the silver candy dish. Then we all drank tea together with a cookie. Oh, it was so *gezellig*!

As Christmas approached each year we polished all the silver in the house—tableware and everything that had to do with Christmas—until it shone. The Christmas table was always tastefully decorated and cheerful.

Tante Betsie had the idea, which became a tradition, of taking tea in bed to every member of the family on Christmas morning. She took me into her confidence about it and gave me a large tray, telling me how she would like it to be set with a cup of tea for everybody and a slice of Christmas bread. And she wanted there to be a lighted candle on the

89

tray. I served everybody, after which I ran back to bed and under the covers because soon the Salvation Army would play Christmas carols behind the towers of the St. Bavo in the early Christmas morning. Everybody in the house always enjoyed hearing these carols while still in bed. We always had wonderful celebrations, especially Christmas, New Year's Eve, *Sinterklaas*, Grandfather's birthday, etc.

There was a very small roof to the Beje, rather like a balcony, next to Grandfather's room. Betsie grew plants there. She tended to them every day. One would have thought they had little chance to grow there, as they received so little sun, but with Betsie's care they thrived. She also took good care of her plants in the parlor. She did this kind of task with a lot of warmth.

Betsie had a strong sense of humor. She laughed a lot when we came from school with silly stories. Sometimes Grandfather told us slang Amsterdam words or popular expressions and Betsie would say, in a pretending official voice, "Now, Father. . . ." But you could see the fun dancing in her eyes.

On New Year's Eve 1891, when Betsie was six years old, Mother ten Boom recorded the following in her diary:

Our Betsie is a lovely girl, sensible in everything. She looks pretty with her long fair curls, and though she is very pale she is in good health. She is hypersensitive and must be treated very carefully because she notices everything and ponders it all. We have to take care that she does not see and hear too much. It is astonishing that she has such a strong memory. Things we have forgotten altogether she remembers exactly with all the details. She is very anxious to learn and carries pencil and paper or slate and slate-pencil with her. She likes this far better than needlework. It is lovely to see how much she enjoys all good things that come her way and how every time she has something special she thanks the Lord for it without you having to tell her to do so. I cannot but say good things of her. She certainly has her faults, but so few that I really should not know what to say about them.

Betsie must indeed have had her faults, but, of course, her family and friends do not describe them. We will, therefore, never know any weaknesses in her character. These descriptions make it hard for me to relate to her because it puts her in a saintlike position. But how could she have been so loved if she were not a real person, just like you and me, with lots of failings?

In 1917, 26 years after her mother described her six-year-old daughter, Betsie showed her true faith in a profound statement that Corrie in her notes described as a simple but serious message for us all. As Europe headed into the final year of the First World War, Betsie said, "It is going to be a harder winter than we have ever had before. We must show through our joy the worth of being a Christian. We should already be doing this, because seeing the dark clouds approaching is often harder than being covered by them."

five

"The Deepest Hell That Man Can Create"

1939–1944

In the late 1930s many in Holland did not recognize the signs of approaching war. Their country had remained neutral in the First World War, and they reckoned that would surely be the case with this war. The Dutch government tried to ignore the signs, assuring the people they did not need to worry because Holland's desire for neutrality would be respected. At the end of 1939 the prime minister assured the people in a radio broadcast that there was absolutely no cause for alarm. He quoted an old Dutch poem, whose author I do not know:

> People often suffer the most
> By anticipating suffering that never happens.
> They, therefore, have more to bear than God gives them to
> bear.

But many did take note of the warning signs. Queen Wilhelmina was one of them. In her autobiography she wrote, "By the spring of 1938, when Hitler invaded Austria, the answer [to the question of what national-socialism would mean for the rest of Europe] was plain to me. German policy would result in a European catastrophe."[1]

As daily life went on, news reports told of one country after another being overtaken by the Germans. In April 1940, Hitler invaded Denmark and Norway.

War!

At three o'clock in the morning of Friday, May 10, 1940, the first German shock troops invaded Holland's most southerly province and took some of the bridges over the river Maas. At the same time a large number of aircraft flew into Dutch airspace. And at about 3:15 a.m. the first ground fighting took place when German soldiers removed the Dutch border patrol in the north of the country to clear the way for an armored German train.

Corrie was jarred awake at about four o'clock by the sound of loud explosions coming from the direction of the airport. In *The Hiding Place* she describes the invasion:

> I sat bolt upright in my bed. What was that? There! There it was again! A brilliant flash followed a second later by an explosion that shook the bed. I scrambled over the covers to the window and leaned out. The patch of sky above the chimney tops glowed orange-red. I felt for my bathrobe and thrust my arms through the sleeves as I whirled down the stairs. At Father's room I pressed my ear against the door. Between bomb bursts I heard the regular rhythm of his breathing.[2]

When she reached her sister's room, Betsie was sitting up in bed. "I groped toward her in the darkness, and we threw our arms around each other. Together we said it aloud: 'War.'"[3]

Holland held out for five days, during which the large port city of Rotterdam was heavily bombed. Soon came a proclamation from the queen that she had decided to take the difficult but urgent step of moving the seat of government away from Holland for as long as necessary. When Corrie heard the queen had left she wept: "I had not cried the night of the invasion but I cried now, for our country was lost."[4] The Netherlands surrendered on May 15, 1940.

During the first year of German occupation, life was fairly normal, but slowly the enemy began to apply restrictions. Nobody was allowed outside after 10:00 p.m. This curfew later was changed to 8:00 p.m., and then 6:00 p.m. Total blackout was ordered. Food was rationed. As time went on radio sets, gold, tin, copper and even bronze church bells had to be handed over to the Germans. The number of people who were allowed to comprise a group was limited. In 1940 the Nazis shut down the Girls' Clubs.

Although attacks on the Jewish population were minor at the beginning of the war, it was not long before the Germans began discriminating against them, starting with the requirement that they all wear a yellow star bearing the word "Jew." Then came attacks on Jewish businesses and synagogues, and they were denied access to shops, restaurants and theaters. Next, the transportations began. Rumors circulated about what might be happening to those who were deported.

Hitler's vision for postwar Europe was that Holland would become a province of Germany. Aryan Dutch men and women who were favorably disposed to Germany would be allowed to stay in Holland. Everybody else would be transported elsewhere. All Jews would be exterminated.

The Underground

By the beginning of 1942 the family at the Beje was involved in underground work. They began finding hiding places for Jewish refugees.

Every Dutch citizen was required to have an identity card on his or her person at all times, and it had to be produced in order to claim ration coupons. As Jewish people began to seek underground addresses it became necessary to obtain coupons and false identity cards for them. These were also needed for the young Dutchmen who otherwise would have been transported to Germany to help with the "labor force."

A very effective motivator, Corrie soon was surrounded by able young Dutchmen whom she called her "boys." They carried out underground errands for her. Willem and Tine's second son, Christiaan, nicknamed Kik, was one of them.

The first to become a refugee in the Ten Boom household was Hans Poley, a young man who came under suspicion of being involved in illegal activities. Having heard of the underground work carried out at the Beje but never having been there, Hans' first meeting with the family was in May 1943:

Carefully following instructions, I turned right into a narrow alley. It was empty, so I pressed the button on the post of the green door. Quick steps sounded and the door opened. "Welcome! Come in, quickly," Corrie's cheerful voice greeted me.

"I am Tante Corrie," she said, "and I do hope you will be very happy here." She led the way, turning left up a short staircase onto another landing where she opened a door into a small room. The curtains were drawn to prevent light from being seen from outside. In the middle was an oval table where a stately lady was busy with her sewing. To the right, next to the stove, sat an older man who could have passed for a patriarch. He had snow-white hair with a beautiful full beard, and he looked at me over his gold-rimmed glasses.

"Father," Tante Corrie said, "this is Hans. He will stay with us for some time." I did not know who to address first—the lady or the obvious master of the house—but he solved the problem. "Well, my boy, we are glad that you trust us to offer you shelter, but we have to expect our ultimate protection from our Father in heaven. We do hope that our Lord will bless your stay. Sit down here."[5]

Barteljorisstraat 19 became a well-known address for illegal activities. It housed refugees, and many underground workers met there to discuss plans and act as couriers. But in spite of the danger and tension of which they were constantly aware, Corrie, Betsie and Father made the best of the situation. They invited their Jewish guests to lead classes in any subjects they might be qualified to teach. They held classes in Hebrew and astronomy, and everyone in the house attended the Italian lessons—including Father, who, always ready to learn a new language, arrived each time with a notebook in his hand. In the evenings the members of the household came together in the living room, sometimes with a wood fire burning, and sang.

A few years later Corrie wrote some notes that describe life in the Beje during the year of 1943:

> As was always the case, there was a happy mood that day. The house where "the three old people lived" was full of the kind of fun caused by the coming together of fourteen people. The overtone was provided by Eusie, who once again was asking whether he really did look very Jewish [or not]. Since there was nothing about him that did not look Jewish, the rest of the company never tired of naming every visible characteristic of his race. Especially Mary and Martha, the two Portuguese Jews, appeared to be very knowledgeable on the subject. There were three young men from Friesland having a meal with us. They had come to Haarlem in connection with their illegal work, and one of them asked how it was possible to keep our work secret from the neighbors when there were such noisy conversations going on.
>
> "First, tell me [if] I would be recognized as a Jew on the street, sir, and then I will tell you how we keep our presence here a secret," replied Eusie.

He had just received the comforting news from his house-mates that he would perhaps be able to walk fifty meters without being recognized as Meyer Mossel, a cantor in the synagogue in Amsterdam, and was about to make up a detailed speech about how the underground activities were kept secret when a ladder was placed against the window and the window cleaner started his work. The curtains were only partly closed, and the man had a good view of the whole company. We were not very pleased with that because we did not know him. It could not be guaranteed that he would keep quiet about what he had seen. Very quickly I, the three Frisian boys, four more boys of their age, our Jewish guests and the others who happened to be in the house at the time conferred with each other about how we could best distract his attention.

It was Eusie who came up with the solution: "Let's act as if it is Tante Betsie's birthday!" Without hesitating for a moment he started to sing that favorite birthday song:

Oh how happy we are today.
It's Tante's birthday, it's Tante's birthday.

The noise level increased, and the window washer could never before have heard a birthday song that could not be finished because of the laughter of the singers. The situation was saved, the size of the group explained. He probably did not notice that Father did not know what to do with himself for laughing and that Betsie could hardly stop her familiar noiseless laugh.

After supper, while those who had to stay inside (those who because of their appearance could not be seen outside) did the washing up, a serious talk took place with the Frisian young men about the technicalities of hiding refugees. They only knew about the hiding places in the farms in the countryside and could not imagine hiding such a large number of people in a city, near the police station and only a short distance from the notorious Nassau Square. What would we do if the Gestapo came?

We were able to calm down the boys. We told them of our system of locks, the opening of which would cause a delay of at least two minutes to anybody wanting to enter the Beje. The house had two doors, one on the main street leading into the shop and one from the alley to the corridor. Both doors had four locks, and if undesirable visitors arrived it was Betsie's job to go to whichever door had been knocked on and fumble with the locks for a while. She was then to maintain that she could not get that door open, but would make her way to the other door, which she surely would be able to open.

In the time that all this took, there was plenty of opportunity to press one of the many buttons that had been placed all over the house. They would cause bells to ring on all three stories. Everybody in the house would hear the alarm signal.

When they heard the alarm bell anybody whose presence in the house could cause difficulties was to go straight to the hiding place in my room. Every refugee was trained to disappear in ninety seconds. If the alarm went at night they first had to fold up their sheets and blankets and turn their mattresses over.

Corrie went on to explain that she and Betsie and Father had given a lot of thought to the situating of the hiding place:

It was quite a long time before we decided upon the false wall in my bedroom. Originally we thought the best place for it would be in a space behind one of the cupboards in the dining room. We worked out that it would hold four people, three sitting down with their backs to the wall with their legs stretched out and the fourth lying across the legs of the other three. But the space was closed off by only a thin partition. Also, as the number of refugees in the house increased, we started to think about a place that might hide them better.

For a short while we experimented with a small space in the attic above the front bedroom. This could be reached only through a hatch high in the wall of another bedroom. In order to help anybody to safety we would have to use the household stepladder. There were too many problems. The older people and the ladies did not want to climb. It would take far too long to hide eight people. Also, the people in hiding would have to make their way through a very narrow passageway past a big beam. We had tried to remove some of the beam with an ax and a saw, but the passageway was still too narrow. Another problem was that there would always have to be somebody in the bedroom to close the hatch after the last refugee was inside, and then that person would have to hang an improbably large etching of the Great Church in The Hague in front of the hatch. So that hiding place was rejected, too.

And then we found the right place. My own bedroom had a blank wall. A second wall was built a short distance from the first wall, and in the left-hand corner of that second wall a cupboard with shelves was built of which the lowest portion of the wooden back of the cupboard could be pushed up. It was ideal. There was room for six to eight people between those two walls.

Ready for use on June 2, 1943, the hiding place was about eight feet long, two feet wide and nearly ten feet high.

The inhabitants of the Beje began to drill with enthusiasm. At the most unexpected and confusing moments Corrie pressed one of the alarm bells. And then a lot of action took place. Nobody wanted to be the last person to disappear into the hiding place. Corrie wrote:

> One cold evening when the whole family had just gone to bed, I pushed the bell for the first night alarm and the droll procession began. Piet was the first to get to the hiding place. He was wearing his pajamas and carrying his clothes. He knelt down somewhat frantically in front of the cupboard, poked his head inside and disappeared. It was as if he had been swallowed by an enormous monster. The last I saw of him was an arm, which reached quickly through the opening to grab his clothes. By this time the others had arrived. One by one they slipped behind the wall from a kneeling position. Eusie came in last, wearing monstrous pajamas with a blue stripe.

Once he was inside I quickly replaced a few boxes and linens on the bottom shelf and closed the sliding panel.

When the practice was completed and the refugees had been given the all clear, they talked about it. There were a few objections. Carrying clothes inside the hiding place cost unnecessary time. It was decided that from then on the refugees would hang their clothes in the hiding place before bedtime. There was also the difficulty about coming out at the end of an alarm. This time I just came into my room and called out "Everything is all right. Come out." But we had heard from acquaintances that sometimes the Gestapo would follow a person suspected of hiding refugees through his house and make him say a sentence like that. We therefore appointed Betsie to knock three times on the panel after every alarm and say: "Come out, children." If they heard any other words the hidden guests were not to raise the panel and were to keep perfectly still.

The "Blow" Comes

September 9, 1943, less than six months before the Beje was raided, Italy capitulated. That evening proved to be one of the busiest the Beje had yet known. The Ten Booms still had a radio because when the Germans demanded all radios be handed over, they had parted with only a very small, spare radio. The main radio was hidden upstairs in the hiding place. The rumor spread quickly through Haarlem that the Italians had given up the fight. People were even beginning to say that the Germans soon would surrender. Since many friends, co-workers and acquaintances knew there was still a radio in the Beje, they came from all sides to hear the great news of the capitulation for themselves. So many people came that it became impossible to listen through the headphones in the hiding place on the third floor and relay the news to the first floor downstairs.

In the end, they brought the radio downstairs and attached the loudspeaker normally used with their record player. Father sat cheerfully in the middle of a group of some thirty people, listening to the news reports that kept streaming in. Happily, there was no raid that evening. "It would have been a big catch for the Gestapo," said Corrie.

Some resistance workers visiting the house for the first time, after hearing about all the happenings at the Beje, would become fearful and act as if they wanted to leave as soon as possible. And Corrie would simply explain, as she did to a nervous courier:

> We do not do these things out of personal bravery. . . . We just live in the belief that God has given us this work, that we understand the danger, but that we know we are hidden under the wings of Him whose care and protection we experience daily.

Toward the end of 1943 the Beje became even more deeply involved with the underground, and a couple of close calls necessitated having to find temporary safer accommodation for the Jews on at least one occasion. In her papers, Corrie tells how all in the Ten Boom household understood the danger of what they were undertaking:

> Father was also completely aware of the possible consequences of our undertakings. We said to him more than once, "You do know, Father, it could happen that we are discovered. Then we will all go to prison and with your poor health you would not survive." Father was 84! He would then go quiet and say that he would obey if God asked him to give his life to protect the old people of the covenant.

The blow came on Monday, February 28, 1944, between five and six o'clock in the evening. Tipped off by a Dutchman who worked as their agent, the Gestapo raided the Beje, which was busy that afternoon. Four Jews were staying as guests, and they were upstairs. Willem had held a Bible study in the dining room, and some of the members had not yet left the house. Nollie also had come to the Beje with her son, Peter, to visit Father. Peter was playing the piano with his back toward two resistance workers who were discussing some plans when the alarm bell sounded. The Jews made straight for the hiding place, and the two resistance workers, whose presence would have aroused suspicion, were pushed up the stairs and through Corrie's bedroom into the hiding place. So the place held Martha, a Portuguese Christian Jew of about 60; Eusie the cantor, about 55; Mary, about 45, a Portuguese Jew; Ronnie, a Jewish young man of about 25; and the two young Dutch resistance workers, Hans and Reynout. Although the family was arrested and the house thoroughly searched, the hiding place was not discovered. After 47 hours those in hiding were released through the cooperation of Dutch police who were sympathetic to the underground and had been informed of the refugees' plight by other resistance workers.

In her papers Corrie describes her thoughts as she, Betsie and Casper were loaded into a police van that would take them away to the Scheveningen prison near The Hague: "In my heart was a great sense of peace. I had long expected this catastrophe. Now the blow had fallen, [and] I accepted it as the close of an exciting chapter of my life. In my mind I kept telling myself, 'Don't ever feel sorry for yourself.'"

Scheveningen

After a journey of about an hour, the doors of the prison closed behind them and Betsie and Corrie were ordered to stand with their faces toward a red brick wall. Father was allowed to sit on a chair. When the sisters' names were called they passed by Casper, who looked up and said his last words to them softly: "The Lord be with you, my daughters." He was to die in prison ten days later.

Corrie was suffering from pleurisy, which was later thought to be tuberculosis, and she was placed in solitary confinement for the three months of their imprisonment at Scheveningen. Betsie was confined in a cell with other women. Although officially they were allowed to write and receive very few letters, some were smuggled in and out, and it is these letters to family and friends that give us insights into prison life. Corrie sometimes wrote brief descriptions of her feelings about life in cell number 384:

> A cell consists of four stone walls and a closed door . . . how greatly a prison deprives people of the most elementary conditions of life. If God still grants me the opportunities, I hope to work in the area of rehabilitation. I will now also dare to visit a prison cell, although I did not dare before now.

Corrie's first letter to "Nollie and all friends" was written on April 11, 1944. She thanks them for the parcel they had sent: "It was perfect! All those colors! I am using the threads from the bath towel to embroider everything." She writes that her main difficulty has been her worry about Betsie and Father, of whom she had heard nothing. She also says, "I am grateful that I am alone, I who love company and people so much! I see my sins more clearly, my own SELF in upper case letters, and I see much more superficiality in myself than I had previously realized. I am continuously looking at Him and trying not to be impatient. I will not be here one minute longer than God deems necessary."

Every two weeks the Red Cross brought packages to the prison for delivery to each prisoner. On one occasion her cell door opened and the prison guard insisted Corrie come and take the package from her even though she was weak with her illness. Remarks Corrie:

> Unkindness is so depressing! I unpack the box. The items are nice and tasty. They were chosen by understanding people who knew what would be good for us. Will this be the last parcel? In another two weeks will we be . . . ?
> Look out, thoughts! It is better to concentrate on and contemplate the Savior. With Him there is certainty. With the

other there is only uncertainty and delayed hope, which hurts the heart.

Betsie was the first to learn of Father's death, but she did not receive that news until a month afterward in a letter from Nollie's daughter Cocky. She wrote back to her niece:

April 11, 1944

Dear Cocky,

So our dear father has been promoted to Glory. The Lord Himself crown his head with the martyr's crown. Many years ago I had a premonition of this, but I steadfastly put it out of my mind. I often thought that a person in whom Christ was shown to such advantage, who lived so close to the Savior, to whom eternal things were so real and who had the gift of prayer in such a wonderful way—such a person had all the conditions for becoming a martyr. And then I would think, *He is not going to die in his bed.* God did not let His sovereignty slip through His fingers. No, this all had to be this way, even my being here in prison. . . .

Cocky, tell everybody who is praying for me that they should especially thank God because miracles are happening here every day. The rush of great waters came to me, but I did not despair for one moment. The Lord is closer to me than ever before in my life. Even in those first terrible days I felt His nearness. I knew that this was not punishment because He suffered completely for me at Golgotha. This horror had come to us from His loving hand to purify me.

Corrie's 52nd Birthday—April 15, 1944

Corrie's birthday came while she was in Scheveningen. Later she recalled:

I was alone, given cold food (nothing hot) and had no opportunity to get fresh air. No books. Everybody was snarling, and I felt so sick and miserable. A doctor gave me a shot, and I told him that it was my birthday and then he gave me a firm handshake. He himself was a prisoner. Never did I appreciate a handshake so much as this one!

Betsie and Corrie were allowed no contact in Scheveningen, and Corrie did not learn of Father's death until three weeks after the news reached Betsie. She wrote to Nollie and family:

His going will leave a great emptiness in my life. The Lord will surely provide many others to whom I can give the love and help I gave him, but that which he gave me can never be replaced. But what a privilege it was that we could enjoy him so intensely for so long. For a few days I was upset. Now that has passed. During the last few days there was such tension inside me. I did not dare to think things through, and when you are so alone it is difficult to get away from your thoughts. Now that is gone and I am thinking much about the future. I am making plans and am experiencing much peace. How good the Savior is to me! He not only bears my burdens, but He carries me, too!

In a letter smuggled out of Scheveningen prison Corrie describes one of the few times she was allowed out of her cell into the fresh air. It is not clear whether while walking in the garden she actually came to the terrible yard she describes or whether she was mentally reliving a description somebody had made of it.

When I had gone through the door it was bolted behind me, and I was alone again. Even in the garden there was only loneliness for those of us sentenced to solitary confinement.

After nine weeks, this was my first time outside. Red flowering shrubs, colorful little primroses, grass, yellow dunes and a wide blue sky. My legs were stinging from their unfamiliar movement, but I walked and walked, on and on, on the rectangular path around the center lawn. I drank in the colors and the air.

Tremendous emotion made my heart beat faster, and then an unspeakable melancholy descended within me. I saw the colors through my tears. In me and around me was more loneliness than in the cell, and all of a sudden I did not see any beauty, just a bare yard, and felt an atmosphere of death and cruelty. At the end, they had dug a long, narrow pit. It looked like a freshly dug grave. Half the shrubs were without leaves and were dead. Around the yard was a high, hard wall with pieces of broken glass in sharp points liberally cemented in its top. And in the north was the tall prison, bare and cold with rows of barred widows. Near the south wall was the gruesome stench of burned bones, and I could hear Kik telling me, "There are already three crematoria in Scheveningen." Behind the south wall the rattle of a machine gun broke the silence. And then, once again, everything was terrifyingly quiet. It was two o'clock and was as if everything around me was a ghost city and I the only one alive. I walked on and an uncontrollable homesickness surged up in my heart.

Then suddenly I remembered Enoch. He was not filled with homesickness when he walked with God, and so I was no longer alone either. God was with me. Hand in hand we walked on and saw the blue sky and the flowers and the flowering shrubs, and I could see the yard as part of a beautiful free world where I would be allowed to walk once again. In the same way, earth is a lonely garden and heaven the liberty where great joy awaits us as children of the light.

Vught

On June 5, the day before D-Day, Betsie and Corrie were reunited when they were suddenly transported from Scheveningen prison to Vught, a German concentration camp in the south of Holland. They were delighted to discover each other while waiting at the railway station for the train that would take them on a slow, twelve-hour journey to their new destination. With many other women prisoners they were placed in a large room, where for the next twelve hours they sat on wooden benches without back rests. They were given neither supervision nor food.

Betsie's diary:

Tuesday, June 6: Unexpectedly brought to Vught in the night to Barrack 4. Corrie and I were together in the train compartment. We enjoyed it immensely. Everything terribly strict here, but still so grateful not to be in a cell any longer.

Thursday, June 15: Transferred into the camp here. We sleep, eat and sew side-by-side and are now so happy! Both had physicals and are fine. Corrie's lungs fully recovered. Must get up at five each morning. Wear overalls and wooden shoes. Have fun walking on wooden shoes. Each day and by night we are experiencing thousands of miracles.

The sisters were assigned tasks at Vught. Betsie's first job was the braiding of heavy ropes, a job so hard on the hands that she eventually was released to lighter duties in the sewing room. Corrie worked in the nearby Phillips factory.

Through every preserved letter shine Betsie's trust, light-heartedness and love. Although often suffering from hunger, she was grateful for the smallest thing and her famous flair for living allowed her to be ever grateful instead of complaining. I cannot find the faintest trace of self-pity in any of her writing.

Sunday, June 25: We had to report to the sewing room. The morning flew by. In the afternoon, fifty of us gathered outside. Wonderful! Then slept and did laundry. In evening, a discussion circle. Nice. Had a wonderful Sunday. Beautiful weather.

Later she expressed thanks for a thimble and a piece of cake given to her by a Belgian woman prisoner:

Yesterday, many blessings. Had a good talk with Smid. Received butter and cheese. Washed a blanket. Cabbage soup. Corrie doing well at Phillips. We enjoy the beauties of nature, the skies, very much. The weather is cold, just right. Every day some sunshine. We receive amazing strength for this harsh life. I am often very hungry. Corrie brings me a warm meal from the factory, and I eat it while we stand at roll call.

On July 6, through a letter from the outside, Betsie and Corrie learned that the Beje and the watch business had been released by the Germans. "We understand that the condition of the house is not bad," wrote Betsie in her diary. "Just what I expected from the Lord."

While Betsie continually displayed such solid faith, joy and even cheerfulness, Corrie's strong imagination and descriptive powers cause us to sense deep emotion in these writings. On August 13, 1944, Corrie wrote to the family:

We are able to witness here and there, but not nearly as much as we had expected. There is much bitterness and communism, cynicism and deep sorrow. The worst for us is not that which we suffer ourselves, but the suffering we see around us. We are learning to put the worst in the hands of the Savior. We are very peaceful, in rather good spirits, but not cheerful. Our health is fine. My hair has turned gray. Life is hard. It is as if I have been drafted into the army but in the harsh German way. But don't worry too much about that. In many aspects it is not too much.

Betsie's letters seem to display a more childlike and pure faith than those of Corrie, as if she was somehow protected from the cruelty, murder and deprivation going on around her. She celebrated—no doubt, for her that is the right word—her 59th birthday on August 19.

Ravensbrück

On September 4 Corrie and Betsie, along with many other women prisoners from Vught, were transported to Ravensbrück concentration camp in Germany on a very slow-moving train. The boxcar should have held about forty women, but eighty were shoved into it. The conditions were terrible; there was no space to sit comfortably, very little water and hardly any fresh air. Tante Corrie told me once that those three long days and nights in the boxcar were the worst time of her ten-month imprisonment.

Ravensbrück was the only major Nazi concentration camp for women, and about twenty European nations were represented there. At the time of Corrie and Betsie's incarceration, the population of the camp was about 80,000. She and Betsie were officially registered as prisoners on September 8, 1944. By the end of the war more than 132,000 women and children had been imprisoned in Ravensbrück, and it is estimated that 92,000 of them died there by starvation, execution or weakness. One of them was Betsie.

The camp authorities forbade any receiving or sending of mail, so we have no written record between the end of August and the end of December, when Corrie was released. (Two dates, December 28 and December 30, appear on her discharge certificates.) But she described the happenings at Ravensbrück in her books *The Hiding Place* and *A Prisoner and Yet . . .*, the latter written early in the year after her release.

In Ravensbrück Betsie and Corrie encountered a world that they had never imagined. Lying, pushing, shoving, filthy words, lice, vermin, starvation, dirt, manipulation and hard labor were their daily lot. Tante Corrie called it "the deepest hell that man can create," where the guards had had "lessons in cruelty."

But God did not allow their spirits to be broken, their love of planning to cease or their prayers to stop. Corrie wrote in *The Hiding Place*:

As we prayed, God spoke to us about the world after the war. It was extraordinary: In this place where whistles and loudspeakers took the place of decisions, God asked us what we were going to do in the years ahead.

Betsie was always very clear about the answer for her and me. We were to have a house, a large one—much larger than the Beje—to which people who had been damaged by concentration-camp life would come until they felt ready to live again in the normal world. She would say, "It is such a beautiful house, Corrie! The floors are all inlaid wood, with statues set in the walls and a broad staircase sweeping down. And gardens! Gardens all around it where they can plant flowers. It will do them such good, Corrie, to care for flowers!"[6]

In the days before her death, Betsie described another phase of the work they would both carry out when they were released. Was she seeing visions or having dreams?

A camp, Corrie—a concentration camp. But we are in charge. The camp was in Germany. It was no longer a prison, but a home where German people who had been warped by his philosophy of hate and force would come to learn another way. There were no walls, no barbed wire and the barracks had window boxes. It will be so good for them . . . watching things grow. People can learn to love from flowers. . . .[7]

Corrie asked Betsie if this camp in Germany was to take the place of the house in Holland. No, Betsie told her, the house in Holland would come first. It was ready and waiting.

As she weakened, Betsie gave new details about that house, and of the barracks in Germany. "The barracks are gray, Corrie, but we will paint them green! Bright, light green, like springtime."[8]

Betsie's final instruction about the future was that she and Corrie would travel the world together. "We must tell people what we have learned here. We must tell them that there is no pit so deep that He is not deeper still. They will listen to us, Corrie, because we have been here."[9] Betsie always spoke in the plural when describing the future to Corrie, who desperately hoped that her sister would indeed live to see the fulfillment of her three dreams. Corrie asked her if they would be together when the work Betsie had described came to pass. "Always together, Corrie! You and I . . . always together."

And in a way they always were together because Betsie's story, forever combined with that of Corrie, would circulate the world. While they were in the camp, Betsie predicted that both she and Corrie would be free by the new year. She passed away on December 16. After her own release two weeks later, Corrie described her anguish at the loss of her sister but then used very comforting words to show us through her eyes her last glimpse of Betsie's face: ". . . full of peace, and happy as a child. She looked incredibly young. The care lines, the grief lines, the deep hollows of hunger and disease were simply gone. In front of me was the Betsie of Haarlem. It was a bit of heaven in the midst of the surrounding hell."[10]

In chapter 4 I quoted an excerpt from one of the letters Tante Corrie received in the last years of her life when she asked for remembrances of Betsie. The letter was from a woman named Jo who had visited the Beje when she was a child. I quoted her perception of the difference between Corrie and Betsie: "It seemed to me that Tante Corrie was the strong one, someone everybody could depend upon wherever that was necessary." But it was the next sentence, which I have saved until now, that really describes much about Betsie: "But it seems that during the war years Betsie was the stronger spiritually." Tante Corrie marked that part of the letter; it surely would have been part of her unwritten book about her sister.

In the coming chapters we will see how Betsie's words were fulfilled through the beautiful house in Holland, the former concentration camp in Germany and the more than three decades of Corrie's world travels.

six

Corrie Begins to Tell Her Story

1945–1947

Corrie was discharged from Ravensbrück concentration camp in the last days of 1944 and made her slow, cold and hungry way by train back to the Netherlands. Germany was in ruins. As the train passed through Berlin she realized that it was New Year's Day 1945. Betsie had been right. They were both free.

Upon her arrival in Holland, Corrie spent ten days in a nursing home in the northern city of Groningen and then stayed two weeks with her brother and family at their home in Hilversum. She was shocked to see that Willem looked very ill and to learn that Kik, the younger of Willem and Tine's two sons who had been active in the underground, had been arrested and sent to Germany. No news of him had been received. But she did learn that the Jews who had been in the hiding place were safe except for Mary, who for some inexplicable reason had gone out into the street shortly after finding another temporary hiding place, where she was arrested and transported to Poland.

Holland was not yet free, and permission to travel was limited. This was also the infamous "Hunger Winter" of 1945, during which, to save themselves from starvation, the Dutch ate even tulip bulbs.

After some difficulty obtaining transportation to her old home-town of Haarlem, Corrie arrived there during the last week of January, delighted to be reunited with Nollie and her family. Then she returned to live in the silent family home.

Home to the Beje

Much had been stolen from the Beje. After the Germans had "unsealed" it during the summer of the previous year it had been used to house homeless families. Four Oriental rugs were gone, as were her typewriter and the clocks and watches left for repair at the time of her arrest. But many priceless things were left, including her piano, the family's Frisian clock and an oil painting of her father given to him as a gift from the people of Haarlem on his eightieth birthday.

Corrie inquired about the many friends and co-workers from the underground work and learned that the group was still operating but on a smaller scale. When she asked about the mentally retarded children and adults she had formerly taught, she learned that their families had hidden them in the back rooms of their houses from the regime that did not think they were "fit to live." Their special schools and institutions had been closed down. Corrie took several of them into the Beje.

All this might be thought enough for a person to undertake in those first few months of recovery from imprisonment, but Corrie was busy with another time-consuming task. She was used to being awakened early in the morning at Ravensbrück for roll call and found that she still automatically awoke long before dawn, unable to return to sleep. Not wanting to waste those hours, she got up and began writing her first book, *Gevangene en Toch . . . (A Prisoner, and Yet . . .)*. Remarkably, this book was ready for the printer by the summer of 1945.

Corrie Begins Telling Her Story

Corrie often described the early days and months after her release as she began to tell others about her experiences. Remembering Betsie's words, "We must tell them, Corrie, what we have learned in this terrible place," she invited all her neighbors to come to the Beje. They all had been very sorry when the Ten Booms were arrested and wanted to know what had happened to Father and Betsie.

As Corrie recounted their experiences, one of the neighbors said, "I am sure it was your faith that carried you through."

"My faith? I don't know about that," replied Corrie. "My faith was so weak, so unstable. It was hard to have faith. When a person is in a safe environment, having faith is easier. But in that camp when I saw my own sister and thousands of others starve to death, where I was surrounded by men and women who had training in cruelty, then I do not think it was my faith that helped me through. No, it was Jesus! He who said, 'I am with you until the end of the world.' It was His eternal arms that carried me through. He was my certainty.

"If I tell you that it was my faith, you might say if you have to go through suffering, 'I don't have Corrie ten Boom's faith.' But if I tell you it was Jesus, then you can trust that He who helped me through will do the same for you. I have always believed it, but now I know from my own experience that His light is stronger than the deepest darkness."

From this beginning, Corrie began to tell her story to anybody in Haarlem who would listen. She rode her bike through the city streets and suburbs to bring the message that when the worst happens in the life of a child of God, then the best remains and the very best is yet to be. Whether she spoke to people individually or in groups, the message was the same, beginning in that Dutch Hunger Winter until the end of her speaking life decades later.

During one of the early meetings in Haarlem, after she had talked about Betsie's vision of a large home for rehabilitation, Tante Corrie was approached by a woman whose face she recognized. She was Mrs. Bierens-de Haan, the owner of a very large house in the wealthy suburb of Bloemendaal. The lady told Corrie that she had five sons, all of whom had fought in the war. Four had returned safely. She believed God had told her during the meeting that if the fifth son came back, she should make her house available for Betsie ten Boom's vision. The fifth son did return and Corrie was invited to visit the house, where she found inlaid wood floors, a sweeping staircase and bas-relief statues set along the walls just as Betsie had described.

On May 5, 1945, the Allies liberated Holland. And at the beginning of June, less than six months after Betsie's death, the beautiful house—named *Schapenduinen,* meaning "Sheep Dunes"—received its first guests. Through the coming years hundreds of people who had suffered mental and physical anguish during the war would receive rehabilitation there and in the larger house that eventually took its place.

For the rest of that year Corrie continued to receive and fulfill many speaking appointments, including one in the city of Nijmegen, where she gave her first talk in English to a group of Canadian servicemen. They told her they hoped she would one day come to speak in their country.

And during that year Corrie told her story to one very significant person. The Dutch collaborator who had betrayed the Beje by tipping off the Germans had been arrested, brought to trial and sentenced to death. His name was Jan Vogel, and Corrie wrote him a letter.

Haarlem, 19 June, 1945

Dear Sir,

I heard today that you are very probably the person who betrayed me. I went through ten months in concentration camp. My father died in prison after ten days and my sister after ten months.

That which you meant for harm, God meant for good for me. I have come closer to Him. A severe punishment is awaiting you. I have prayed that the Lord will accept you if you turn to Him. Remember that the Lord Jesus bore your sins, too, on the cross. If you accept that and want to be His child, you will be saved for eternity.

I have forgiven you everything. God will forgive you, too, if you ask Him. He loves you and sent His Son to earth to pay the price for your sins—to bear the punishment for you and me. You need to give an answer to that. When He says, "Come to Me, give Me your heart," then your answer must be, "Yes, Lord, I want to. Make me Your child."

If you find it difficult to pray, ask if God will give you His Spirit. He will give faith in your heart.

Never doubt the love of the Lord Jesus. He is waiting to receive you with outstretched arms.

I hope that the deep path you now must take will work toward your eternal salvation.

Sincerely,
Corrie ten Boom

To America on Fifty Dollars

It is not clear who suggested to Corrie that she visit the United States to tell her story, but she quickly made plans to go there. She saw it as God's guidance in fulfillment of Betsie's dream that they would go around the world with their story. In her diary on January 26, 1946, she recorded:

> Planning a foreign trip is wonderfully exciting, and for me it is doubly wonderful because it is such a contrast with my last foreign journey. Then I was being taken against my will to the land of the enemy, but now by my own free will I am going on an evangelization journey through a friendly country. What an adventure! I know so little about what is awaiting me. I will have $50 with me and some notes of introduction, but I do not know anybody there. What a privilege to have been called to evangelize in another part of the world—I, a weak, sinful, little person. But I know that God's power is made perfect in weakness. I experienced that in the camps.

Leaving the rehabilitation center in the hands of a Dutch board and a caring staff, Corrie moved on to the next challenge. After considerable difficulty in obtaining her visa, Corrie left Holland for America on a cargo ship. Fifty dollars was all she was allowed to take out of the country. An American businessman whom she had met in Holland, however, had given her two checks, one small and one somewhat larger, for her to use if necessary. "You can pay me back later," he said.

Arriving in New York City, Corrie went to the YWCA and found a room. One of the addresses she had been given in Holland was that of a group of Christian Jews who had immigrated to America and held meetings in New York City. She called them and learned that they were from Germany. They invited her to speak to them, but the English speaking notes she had made on the trip across the Atlantic Ocean could not be used. Her first talk in the United States was in German.

After staying at the YWCA for a week, she received a letter from somebody who had heard her speak at the Jewish meeting. Knowing how difficult it was to find rooms in New York, this lady whom she had never met offered Corrie the use of a room in her house. She accepted quickly and became the woman's guest for the next five weeks.

Corrie spent her days looking up the addresses she had been given in Holland. The Americans were polite and some seemed interested, but nobody asked her to speak. She even began knocking on the doors of churches, offering to tell her story. But few people were interested. After a couple of weeks she began to run out of money. Her daily food for some time was what she described to me as "a Nedick's breakfast." It cost ten cents and consisted of a cup of coffee, a doughnut and some orange juice.

"One day on that first visit to New York," she recalled to me late in her life, "I met some American girls. They invited me to have lunch with them as their guest. I had chicken and gravy and potatoes and vegetables. Oh, it tasted so good. That day I started to love the Americans!"

As the weeks progressed, Corrie felt increasing resistance to her message. Nobody was interested in an older Dutch woman who wanted to give talks. Nor did they seem to understand that there was such a thing as God's guidance.

"But God's guidance is much more important than common sense. I know He has told me to give this message in America. I can tell from my own experience that the light of Jesus is stronger than the deepest darkness."

"We have ministers to tell us that," was the response.

"Of course you have. But from my own experience I can tell people that what the ministers say is true."

"It would have been better if you had stayed in Holland. We don't need any more preachers. Too many Europeans are coming to America. Something should be done about it."[1]

After five weeks of no work Corrie was beginning to wonder if she should indeed return to Holland, when the first of a chain of events took place that were to lead to open doors all over the United States. First, she met a Dutch minister who had heard about her story. She stayed with his family in the pastoral manse for five days: "What a joy to eat good Dutch food again." A week later after a service in a different church she met Irving Harris, editor of the magazine *The Evangel*. He was interested in her story and asked if she had any written material he could publish in his magazine. She gave him a copy of one of her lectures and before they parted, Mr. Harris gave her the name and phone number of a Mr. Abraham Vereide in Washington, D.C. Reluctant at first, Corrie finally called Mr. Vereide and received a warm invitation to come to Washington.

More Than Sufficient Work

Twenty-five years later Corrie wrote about Mr. Vereide in her news magazine *It's Harvest Time*.

In the U.S.A. I started to bring the Gospel, but no doors were open to me until I met Abraham Vereide. He introduced me to many people. It was my joy to work with him in the International Christian Leadership Breakfast Groups. Abraham was a man full of the joy of the Lord, always prepared to tell everyone about Jesus, whom he loved. His introductions were always unusual. Once I was with a group of highly educated people. Abraham did not forget the title of any of the people in the group. I wondered how he would introduce Corrie ten Boom, just a licensed watchmaker. Without hesitation he said with a smile, "Corrie ten Boom was graduated from the University of Ravensbrück." It certainly had been training in that prison camp! I was still more moved when he put his arm around my shoulders and said, "Corrie ten Boom, God's own girl."

From that time on, Corrie had more than sufficient work. Soon she was able to pay back the businessman who had given her the two checks "to use if necessary." Something of the scope of her new work is shown through some notes she made in Toronto on June 2, 1946: "It is no small thing to be put to work in Canada. I see so many possibilities that I could stay for the rest of my life in Toronto and have enough work. In the last fourteen days I have held 24 talks, four newspaper interviews and a radio interview."

During her time in Canada she met a Mrs. Bobbie Halliday from whom she received much kindness through the coming years, not the least of which was the supply of clothes. When I started traveling with Tante Corrie in 1976 she told me that according to Mrs. Halliday she had only one dress on her first visit to America. "But," said Corrie to me thirty years later, "I cannot have had just one dress. I must have been wearing one and had another in my suitcase."

She began to write letters in English from time to time, which were mimeographed and sent to the new friends she had made, and she kept in touch with her Dutch friends through a column in a Dutch evangelical magazine. Because Mrs. Halliday kept copies of these letters we are able to follow Corrie's early travels with some accuracy.

The first of these letters, which I have been able to track down, was written from Prairie View, Kansas, on July 15, 1946, about four months after she met Abraham Vereide. Among other places where she had already spoken were New York City, Philadelphia, Washington, D.C., Staten Island, Vermont, Ottawa, Toronto, Detroit and Grand Rapids. She must have already shared with some of those new friends her difficulty in understanding Americans and her lack of fluency in English, for she said:

> The language difficulty is no more a real brake upon the work, or [my] not understanding the American people. I accept them now as they are. When they are different from the Dutch I don't judge but try to understand their elementary needs. To many thousands I brought the message during the last months . . . thirty lady lawyers at a dinner of the Women's Bar Association at Chicago accepted me extraordinarily. A Jewish Women's Congress did not accept me at all, and one asked me: "Why did you speak of Jesus? Did you not know that you were speaking to Jews?" I certainly did.

Underneath the mimeographed letter, Corrie added a note in her own handwriting: "Your dress, Bobbie, is a real blessing. I am sure that I am quite ladylike with it . . . when I spoke for the lady lawyers I was so glad I had that dress."

Two months later, in October 1946, after having spoken in California and Utah and 22 times in Iowa, Corrie wrote:

My health is splendid, and in my heart is an ever-growing joy. To bring the light makes you so happy. It shines into your own heart . . . to everyone I may tell about the victory of Christ! How good it is to know that all work in God's Kingdom is for His sake. Jesus works in our hearts the love of God by His Holy Spirit (Romans 5:5). What rich children of the King we are! Why do we so often live like beggars?

How do people respond? Sometimes they tell me I come over too strongly. I think they say that because I see more and more that we may not be content with living as if we are only partly a child of God. Sometimes God's Spirit shows the people their sins and brings them to the happy deed of giving their life to Him. Some have been strengthened by my telling of the small and large miracles God did and does in my life and dare now bring their own difficulties to Him. Yes, God does miracles even now in my life. Is it not a miracle that I might give more than 160 lectures and I am not tired?

On December 14 I hope to leave on the *Queen Elizabeth* for England and then be home at Christmas.

Corrie had much to do, however, in the intervening two months. On November 19 she wrote to Abraham Vereide requesting his prayers and the use of his influence to free Hans Rahms, a German judge at Scheveningen who tried to secure Corrie and Betsie's freedom after their arrest. He was then interred in Germany.

Will you try to get free Hans Rahms, at Hammelburg bei Bad Kissingen 9793 Internment Camp in Germany?

In April 1944 he questioned our family, set free 32 people who were in prison with us. He knew that most of them were underground workers. He changed my Protocol and tried in several ways to set free my sister and me but did not succeed because another judge got our trial. Hans Rahms listened with real interest when we spoke of the Gospel and allowed my sister to pray with him. When it is useful, I will take him in our house in Holland for a time with his family. Will you get permission for that? Pray that they may be saved for eternity.

In the same letter to Mr. Vereide she wrote: "People say that Molotov [the Soviet foreign minister] will be on the *Queen Elizabeth* on December 14. Pray that I may bring him my message. God is a God of miracles."

Because there is no further mention of Molotov, it seems that she was not able to bring him her message. But as for Hans Rahms, he must have been released because several years later she renewed her acquaintance with him on a visit to Germany and explained the Gospel and his need of the Lord Jesus as his Savior. Rahms accepted Him and later she wrote, "I know his sins were forgiven and that his name was written in the Book of Life."

Home Again

From that first of countless travels abroad, Corrie arrived back in the Netherlands shortly after the death of her brother, Willem, who passed away in December 1946 of tuberculosis of the spine, contracted in prison. Just before he died, Willem opened his eyes to tell Tine, "It is good, it is very good, with Kik." Although they had long surmised that Kik was no longer alive, not until 1953 did the family receive confirmation that he had died in 1945 in Bergen-Belsen concentration camp.

Father, Betsie, Willem and Kik—four Ten Booms—had given their lives for shielding and saving Jewish refugees.

seven

"We Are Able to Live as King's Children"

1947–1953

*C*orrie's home in Holland was now the beautiful rehabilitation center in Bloemendaal near Haarlem. It was to her room there that she returned from her ten-month adventure in the United States.

One of her first tasks was to tell the Dutch Christians what she had learned in America. Just as the Ten Boom family, under Father's example, had looked for and received fellowship and instruction from Christians outside their own denomination, Corrie showed the same spirit to her new friends across the Atlantic in a circular letter dated June 27, 1947:

> It is half a year since I left America. How much that time in your country has meant to me! All you many people I know are my friends who pray for me.

Amongst other things my work in Holland has been to tell people here what I learned in America. For example, I tell them about Youth for Christ, about Breakfast Groups, about the Christian Businessmen's Committee, about the Gideons, to show them how America understands the mission call. It inspires the Dutch. I hope that people here will get the same spirit of action. Many people in Holland have a wrong idea about America, just as I had before I visited you. During my trip through your country I learned to love the American people.

The house in Bloemendaal had been open for a year. Corrie wrote:

Most of the war victims are back into society. Now all sorts of tired people needing a period of rest spiritually and physically can come to the beautiful house with its large park. We also held eight conferences during a two-month period for young people who want to use their spare time for the spreading of the Gospel.

We need a far bigger house where we can have longer conferences, a Bible-school, a retreat and rehabilitation home at the same time. We know that God will give us the house and the money we need for it at His time.

In July 1947 she wrote to Bobbie Halliday, her clothes supplier from Canada:

My dear Bobbie,

Today I wear the green dress you gave me last year! So often I think of you, also during the winter when in the cold I had your nice warm cardigan.

Like most effective Christian leaders, Corrie read a lot. Until a stroke took her ability to read when she was in her mideighties, she read avidly with an attitude that always wanted to learn. Her letter to Bobbie continued:

Did I send you the book *In His Presence* by Kenyon? This book gave me much blessing. Write if you did not get it, and I will send it. I cannot believe everything that is in it, but it gave me much light and made Jesus' victory more real for me. We *are* God's children. We may go to God's throne every moment of the day or night. We have legal rights to take all the promises of the Bible. Demons reign over us by bluff; they have no real power. Perhaps they have a little bit, but the power of Jesus is far and far greater.

Then she made a request to Bobbie:

My house "Schapenduinen" is blessed. It is not large enough, and there is a chance I can get an unfurnished house where people can sleep in their own rooms. Can you perhaps help me by sending curtains or tablecloths? In America I saw those cotton bags for chicken food. Could you get them? Don't worry if you can't. God will take care of everything.

A Face from the Past in Germany

In the latter part of 1947, nearly three years after her release from imprisonment, Corrie went back to Germany. It was then that she had an encounter with one of her former guards. Those who know Corrie's story probably have heard the following many times, but I would not be true to her memory if I did not include this vital part of her message—forgiving our enemies:

It was at a church service in Munich that I saw him, the former SS man who had stood guard at the shower room door in the processing center at Ravensbrück. He was the first of our actual jailers that I had seen since that time. And suddenly it was all there—the roomful of mocking men, the heaps of clothing, Betsie's pain-blanched face.

He came up to me as the church was emptying, beaming and bowing. "How grateful I am for your message, Fraulein," he said. "To think that, as you say, He has washed my sins away."

His hand was thrust out to shake mine. And I, who had preached so often to the people in Bloemendaal the need to forgive, kept my hand at my side. Even as the angry, vengeful thoughts boiled through me, I saw the sin of them. Jesus Christ had died for this man; was I going to ask for more? *Lord Jesus, I prayed, forgive me and help me to forgive him.*

I tried to smile, and I struggled to raise my hand. I could not. I felt nothing, not the slightest spark of warmth or charity. And so again I breathed a silent prayer. *Jesus, I cannot forgive him. Give me your forgiveness.*

As I took his hand, the most incredible thing happened. From my shoulder and along my arm and through my hand a current seemed to pass from me to him while into my heart sprang a love for this stranger that almost overwhelmed me.

And so I discovered that it is not on our forgiveness any more than on our goodness that the world's healing hinges, but on His. When He tells us to love our enemies, He gives, along with the command, the love itself.[1]

I heard Corrie tell this story at every meeting to which I accompanied her. She gave this example of the importance of forgiveness for 33 years throughout the world.

1948–49

It was estimated that nine million people were without homes in postwar Germany. They were living on bombed sites, in half-standing houses and in heaps of rubble. Corrie was invited by a church group to speak to and work among one hundred families living in an abandoned factory building. Sheets and blankets divided each family's living space from the next in an attempt to provide some kind of privacy, but it was not possible to escape the sounds of babies crying, radios set at high volume or family squabbles. Corrie decided that in order to bring her message of the victory of the Lord Jesus she needed to thoroughly identify with the homeless people and live as they lived, not returning to the hostel room outside the city that the church had provided for her. After she had been living in the abandoned factory for several months, the director of a relief organization came to see her. He had heard about her rehabilitation work in Holland and wanted her to start something similar in Germany.

"We've located a place for the work," he told her. "It is a former concentration camp that has just been released by the government."

She drove with him to Darmstadt to see the camp. Rolls of rusting barbed wire still surrounded it, and a cinder path led to gray barrack buildings. But in her mind's eye Corrie saw something else. Betsie's dream was about to be turned into reality. I have before me a photograph of those buildings after they had been prepared to receive German people in need. They are clean and neat and painted spring-green. And there are window boxes.

These activities were interspersed with much travel. Although not many records of her comings and goings in 1948 exist, we know that she spent April 15, her 56th birthday, in Los Angeles, where she was speaking to students at the University of California. The student who acted as her chauffeur on that day later wrote:

> She taught me what the true love of Jesus Christ can do in the life of a chosen vessel. Her spiritual depth and insight into Biblical truths, coupled with the compassionate understanding that had come from her time in a Nazi concentration camp, left me with the desire to do more with my life than just earn a good living.

Before the end of 1949, five years after her death, Betsie's dreams had already been established for several years, and a larger reha-bilitation house in Holland had been acquired. This is confirmed in another letter Corrie wrote just before Christmas that year to her friends in America and Canada.

> After seven months in Germany and the rather rough crossing in the freighter, I had lost weight but gained it very soon in this land of plenty.
>
> From Holland, Bloemendaal, good news. The house, Zonneduin (meaning "Sun Dune"), bought in faith, had to be altered. We have now 28 beds. It is a home for people who need a time of rest—house mothers, patients who had to leave the hospitals but are not yet able to do their work, and many different kinds of people who find there a home with good nursing and—what is the most important—come in contact with the Gospel of Jesus Christ. The builders were not yet paid and telephoned that if we did not pay that week they should go to a lawyer. The lady director said, "Then I go to my heavenly lawyer." She went on her knees and told the Lord that there was no money to pay. The next day our Queen Juliana sent 4,000 guilders, about $1,300. So the King of kings moved a queen to help us out.
>
> In Germany, the former concentration camp where we have now 85 refugees, the barracks had to be painted and the walls here and there strengthened. We hope that the barracks will be less drafty now in the coming winter. One hundred forty refugees left to live now in their own built houses.

"Let Us Expect Much—Then God Gives Much"

In October 1950 Corrie wrote to her friends that she had arrived back in Holland in August. Tante Corrie always had a great sense of urgency:

> It seems as if the world is going down. We know it is. Romans 8:19: "The creation waits in eager expectation for the sons of God to be revealed." Knowing this, let us use our time

not in straightening pictures in a house on fire but jumping into the work of saving souls, losing our lives for Jesus' sake and thus finding them. Not with sad faces, but filled with the Holy Spirit and joy, knowing that Jesus not only cures but also renews. We have a Savior who not only died for our sins, but the moment He went to sit at the right hand of the Father He began to live for us. The devil accuses us night and day but our advocate, Jesus, says that we are God's righteousness in Him.

So we are able to live not like beggars, but as King's children—yes, God's children. Tell that to the devil; that is the best way to resist him. Act on the Word of God; you will experience that it is true. A believer is a possessor. Let us expect much—then God gives much. Let us not try to live a resurrection-life with Christ without following Him in His death. Then He can fill us with His love, which is victorious over all circumstances.

In December 1951 Corrie wrote again to Bobbie Halliday, who continued to keep her supplied with dresses:

O, that your prayers for me may be answered and that God may use me to "ignite the spark into flame," like you wrote. I am thankful but not satisfied. I have so many opportunities. Pray that I may be used one hundred percent everywhere. "Streams of living water" is what I pray for.

The Weaver

In February 1952 Corrie received a letter from the superintendent of the American Board of Missions to the Jews. It contained a poem called *The Weaver* by Grant Colfax Tullar, which from then on Corrie frequently quoted.

She used the poem in a very special way. Corrie liked to use visual aids in her work, and one principal aid was her crown

Corrie begins her travels, U.S.A., 1946   PHOTO COURTESY OF THE CORRIE TEN BOOM HOUSE FOUNDATION

embroidery. She often used it to help her audiences see their circumstances "a little bit from God's point of view."

She would begin, "When the worst happens in the life of a child of God—and for me it did—the best remains and the very best is yet to be." Then she would slip out of her bag a piece of shiny blue cloth which, you may recall from chapter 1, when she and I were packing for our first journey together I had mistaken for embroidery. She would hold it up backward so that the audience found themselves staring at the tangled, knotted, untidy, yellow threads on the underside of the cloth, and she would quote *The Weaver:*

> My life is like a weaving
> Between my God and me.
> I do not choose the colors;
> He worketh steadily.
>
> Ofttimes He chooseth sorrow,
> And I in foolish pride
> Forget He sees the upper
> And I the underside.

As she spoke the last two lines, Corrie would turn the cloth around so everybody would see a golden crown instead of tangled threads, and she would continue:

> Not till the loom is silent
> And the shuttles cease to fly
> Will God unroll the canvas
> And explain the reason why.
>
> The dark threads are as needful
> In the skillful Weaver's hand
> As the threads of gold and silver
> In the pattern He has planned.[2]

A Blessed Life

In 1952 Corrie made her first visit to Japan. On her sixtieth birthday, April 15, 1952, Corrie wrote to Bobbie Halliday from the YWCA in Tokyo:

The weeks and days before leaving the States were full and fuller up 'til the last evening. Then I spent four days in Honolulu, where I spoke *sixteen* times. A time of great blessing, and I

Corrie at 60 years of age in Japan, 1952,   PHOTO COURTESY OF THE CORRIE TEN BOOM HOUSE FOUNDATION
with missionary Mrs. Mitchell

was not tired at all. . . . Japan is different from anything else. I preached Sunday and had to leave my shoes outside.

And in November 1952:

I traveled over the northern island of Japan. Here I learned to know the real Japanese life. Sleeping, eating and living in Japanese style was very interesting but not always easy for an old girl like I am. But the Lord gave me much strength. When my weakness leans on His might, all seems light. Thank you for your prayers and help! Yes, Ravensbrück was a good training. Sometimes when I sleep on a dirty bed on the floor in a small hotel far away in the country, I say to myself, "Ravensbrück was worse."

Corrie worked in Japan for nine months. Although she believed God had called her to proceed to Taiwan, New Zealand and South Africa, lack of funds for the journey prevented her leaving Japan when she had hoped.

But Corrie knew the joy of trusting in the Lord with a faithful heart, and this became very evident when she referred to her financial needs in her letters during this time. By now Corrie had a mailing list of thousands of people. In one letter she wrote:

> Friends often ask questions and want to know more about the various projects that are supported by the funds I receive, so I will tell you about them and their prayer needs.
>
> First, there is the International Home, Zonneduin in Holland. The small charge of two dollars a day, which includes meals, does not cover the cost of running such a home; yet it has been a haven of rest to many who could not pay even that much.
>
> Second, there is the former concentration camp in Darmstadt, Germany, where 85 refugees are living while they work and build their own homes. When they move out, others take their place. This camp often needs repairs, in addition to helping these people become established.
>
> Third, there is the sending of these newsletters to about 18,000 in fifteen different countries. Pray that the Lord will bless this letter and for the other people on my mailing list. Many have spiritual needs, and about a thousand are prisoners.
>
> Fourth, there are my expenses to carry the message that Jesus is Victor around the world. Thanks to all the dear people who, as Phillips translates Romans 12:13, "never grudged me a bed or a meal." I seldom have to use God's money for personal expenses. Traveling from place to place is always the big item.

Although Corrie told her audiences about the financial needs for her rehabilitation house in Holland and for the work in Germany, she never asked for money for herself.

She did eventually continue with her planned trip into other parts of Asia. From Taiwan in January 1953, after describing her work there, she wrote:

> I told you here a little snapshot of my life. What a blessed life I have! In churches, streets, prisons, Bible schools and missionary meetings, God uses me. Late in the evenings I am tired, but God gives me always a healthy sleep each night, and then I am peppy again. The joy of the Lord is my strength [see Nehemiah 8:10].
>
> Is it always easy? No. Of course, I have moments that the spirit of self-pity asks entrance into my heart. One day recently cockroaches ate holes in my dress, the dirty scoundrels. I try to travel light and have not too many dresses with me, and just that day I had no money to pay my room, though it was no high amount at all. I also needed money for my air ticket, for the letters to my mailing lists in America and Japan. I did not really worry but asked God, "May I tell my friends about my shortage of money?"
>
> The Lord answered only, "Trust Me!" I was so very happy about that answer and went to bed wondering how the Lord should help me out this time.
>
> The next day was very busy, and I came home very late. For the first time mail reached me in Taiwan. There were 36 letters. The first I opened had a check of $150, and then there was a letter from [my representative in the U.S.] to tell me about many Christmas gifts for me in money. I had money for every need of that moment, even for the air tickets. It is no risk to trust the Lord. Faith is a problem for those who do not know the Lord and the Word.
>
> Does that mean always answered prayers? Surely not, although no problem is too great or too small for the Lord, and He is far more ready to answer our prayers than we are ready to pray. Sometimes He allows deep ways.

eight

In the Power
of the Holy Spirit

1954–1959

On October 22, 1953, Corrie's beloved sister Nollie died at the age of 63. Away from Holland at the time, Corrie received the news by telegram. In a letter to her friends she wrote:

That afternoon Nollie had had a Bible study group at her home. In the evening she passed away, only one step from earth to heaven. What a joy for her to be with the Lord. For me earth is much emptier, heaven still fuller. Nollie went a train earlier. Not lost, but gone before.

Nollie wrote to me every week. We were very much united in the Lord. Three letters reached me still after her death. She helped me often with good illustrations. In one of her letters she wrote:

A king gave a little golden staff to his jester and said, "Keep this staff till you find a greater fool than you are, and then give it to him." When the king was dying, the jester came to him. "I am going on a long journey to a country far away," said the king. The jester answered, "But I do not see any suitcases. Did you not make any preparations?" "No," said the king, "I made neither reservations nor preparations." Then the jester gave him the little staff and said, "Now I have found a greater fool than I am."

Is not that a good one? By the way, how about you? Read 1 John 5:11–13.

A Turning Point

Shortly after Nollie's death came a turning point in Corrie's ministry—such an extraordinary one that her countenance changed. When I look at photographs of her from before and after that year, 1954, I see that she was given an unusual empowerment to continue her work. Her face had a new radiance and love, and it remained there until the end of her life. It began with a puzzling time. It is best that she tell the story in her own words:

As I stood in the railroad station in Basel, Switzerland, waiting for my luggage, I suddenly realized that I did not know where I was supposed to go. For the eight years after my release from prison, I had been traveling all over the world at the direction of God. Many times I did not know why I was to go to a certain place until I arrived. It had become almost second nature not to make my plans and then to ask for God's signature. Rather, I had learned to wait for God's plan and then write my name on the schedule.

But this time was different. Suddenly I was in Basel and had no idea why or who I was to contact. Besides, I was tired. Sleeping each night in a different bed and always living out of a suitcase had worn me down. I felt a sensation of panic in my heart and sat down, trying to remember to whom I was going. At 61 years of age, could it be that I was so overworked that I was losing my memory? Or even worse, had God withdrawn His conscious Presence from me and was letting me walk alone for a season?

In my suitcase I found an address. It had no meaning to me, but it was all I had to go on. I took a taxi to the place, but the people at that address were complete strangers and had never heard of me. By now I was desperate—and a little bit frightened. The people told me of another man I might contact. Perhaps he would know who I was and why I had come to Basel. I took another taxi, but this gentleman, too, was unfamiliar with my work.

For eight years the Lord had guided me step by step. At no time had I been confused or afraid. Now I was both—unable to recognize the Presence of God. Surely He was still guiding me, but like the pilot who flies into the clouds I now was having to rely on instruments rather than sight. I decided to turn around and go back home to Holland, there to await further orders.

Because of a severe storm, the planes were not flying. I had to travel by train. Arriving in Haarlem, I started toward the phone near the station to call our rehabilitation house in Bloemendaal where I was to stay. But on the way to the phone booth I slipped on the wet pavement, and before I knew it I was sprawled in the street. A sharp pain shot through my hip, and I was unable to stand.

"Oh, Lord," I prayed, "lay Your hand on my hip and take away this horrible pain." Instantly the pain disappeared, but I was still unable to get up. Kind people assisted me to a taxi, where a policeman asked if he could help.

"What is your name?" he asked.

"Corrie ten Boom."

He looked surprised and questioned me further. "Are you a member of the family of that name whom we arrested during the war?"

"That is right."

During the war, many Dutch policemen had stayed in the service of the Gestapo, not as traitors but for the express purpose of helping political prisoners. This man had been on duty that day my family was arrested.

"I am so sorry about your accident," he said sympathetically, "but I am glad to see you again. I will never forget that night in the police station. You all were sitting or lying on the floor of the station. Your old father was there with all his children and many of your friends. I have often told my colleagues that there was an atmosphere of peace and joy in our station that night, as if you were going to a feast instead of prison and death."

He paused and looked at me kindly as if trying to remember my face. "Your father said before he tried to sleep, 'Let us pray together.' And then he read Psalm 91."

"You remember!" I exclaimed. After eight years that policeman had remembered which psalm my father had read. For a fleeting moment, sitting in that old taxi on a Haarlem street while the rain pelted the roof, I allowed myself the pain of looking backward. It was in this same city that we had been arrested. In fact, the prison was only a short distance from where I was sitting. That was the last time our family had been together. Within ten days Father was dead. Then later Betsie. All gone. And this policeman still remembered.

"He who dwells in the shelter of the Most High will rest in the shadow of the Almighty" (Psalm 91:1). Now the message was clear. Although there was no light to guide me, I was still in God's will. Actually, when one is resting (abiding) under the shadow of the Almighty there will be no light, but that is only because God's Presence is so near.

I leaned back in the seat. "Dear God, when this shadow came over me I thought you had departed. Now I understand it was because you were drawing closer. I eagerly await whatever you have planned for me."

Eager I was, but not so patient. An x-ray showed my hip was not broken, only badly bruised. The doctor said I would have to remain in bed for several weeks for it to heal. . . . I was put to bed in Zonneduin, our rehabilitation house, unable to move or turn over without the help of a nurse.

I was a very impatient patient. I had only five days to get to a student conference in Germany, and as the days slipped by and I realized my hip was not healing fast enough to make the conference, I grew irritable.

"Is there not a Christian in all Haarlem who can pray for me to be healed?" I asked. My friends sent for a particular minister in the city who was known to have laid hands on the sick for healing. That same afternoon he came to my room. Standing beside my bed he asked, "Is there any unconfessed sin in your life?"

What an odd question, I thought. I understood he had agreed to come pray for my healing, but was it his job to get so personal about my sins and attitudes? However, I did not have far to look. My impatience and the demanding attitude I had displayed toward my nurse had been wrong—very wrong. I asked her to come to the room and I repented of my sin, asking both her and God to forgive me.

Satisfied, this gentle man then reached over and laid his hands on my head. Only a few months earlier, my sister Nollie had died. Ever since my heart had been broken with mourning. I had the feeling of being left all alone and knew that the insecurity I had experienced had contributed to my being here in this bed, rather than in Germany with the students. Yet as this tall, handsome man laid his hands on me and prayed, I felt a great stream of power flowing through me. Such great joy. The mourning left, and I wanted to sing with David, "Thou hast turned for me my mourning into dancing: thou hast put off my sackcloth, and girded me with gladness" (Psalm 30:11, KJV).

I felt the Presence of the Lord Jesus all around me, and I felt His love flowing through me and over me as if I were being immersed in an ocean of grace. My joy became so intense that I finally prayed, *No more, Lord, no more.* My heart felt it was about to burst, so great was the joy. I knew it was that wonderful experience promised by Jesus—the Baptism in the Holy Spirit.[1]

The Holy Spirit

Corrie did not use the term "baptism in the Holy Spirit" exclusively. She talked about the "fullness of the Holy Spirit." She taught the people, "The question is not whether you have the Holy Spirit [or not], but whether the Holy Spirit has you." A strongly grounded member of the Dutch Reformed Church, she knew that it is only through the Holy Spirit that a person can receive the Lord Jesus Christ. He comes to each person at his or her conversion. But she strongly believed that it was possible for a person to be only partly full of the Holy Spirit. She prayed for the fullness of the Holy Spirit every day and often said that Ephesians 5:18 contained the most joyful commandment of the Bible: "Be filled with the Spirit." And each time she used that text in her talks she explained that the Greek tense of the verb means "be being filled"—a continuous state.

After her hip healed, Corrie made her way to Germany for her speaking appointments, and she said she was "still filled with joy overflowing." It was only after she arrived that she realized why God had chosen that particular time to fill her with His Holy Spirit:

> For in Germany, for the first time, I came face-to-face with many people who were demonized. Had I gone in my own power I would have been consumed. Now, going in the power of the Holy Spirit, God was able to work much deliverance through me as we commanded demons to be cast out in the name of the Lord Jesus Christ.[2]

Hidden Behind the Cross

All through the 1950s, Corrie traveled and spoke constantly. Her journeys usually were made alone. When she and I first began to travel together in 1976 she told me she was glad she had a companion. "In the first years of my work I went around the world twice—six years each time. It was often lonely. Sometimes I bought a *Reader's Digest* for company as I left my new friends and journeyed to the next country," she said.

Corrie was completely undenominational. She worked with every leader who loved the Lord Jesus. At the beginning of 1955 she wrote to her friends that she was working in Canada "with much joy." She went on:

> God blesses the work very much. My schedule is very full, but the Lord is my strength. I speak not only in many different churches, but also in jails, universities, men's and ladies' clubs, high schools, etc. I am really ecumenical. Today I spoke in an Anglican church and wore a robe of a Baptist minister, and with me Dutch Reformed, I thought that was pretty good.

Corrie was also able to relinquish a work she had started but could not complete. She described an instance in Darmstadt, Germany, where she already had the camp for German refugees:

> There was a Deaconess House there that needed help to rebuild a ruined refugee home for girls. I had then just enough money to have the ruins removed and the foundation and basement built. Now I have a photo of the house, built and ready to use. So sometimes God uses me to start a work that I cannot finish but gives vision and courage to the people to go on.

Corrie also seemed almost indefatigable. In May 1955, having arrived to speak at Dr. Tozer's church in Chicago a few hours early, she took the opportunity to write to her friends:

> In Canada I had to have a little operation and was a week in the hospital. I took it easy afterward, during ten days, by speaking not more than once a day and doing little traveling. But now the Lord has renewed my strength and healed me one hundred percent. My schedule is now, God willing, June and July, Mexico, August–October, west coast of America from Vancouver to San

Diego. Pray much for me, will you? Pray that people who hear me may forget the channel, seeing only Him. Pray that Corrie ten Boom may be hidden behind the cross of Jesus.

Corrie received the voluntary help of secretaries during her stays in various cities and sometimes for a portion of her travels:

For the last quarter of 1955 God gave me a very good secretary who has now returned to her home in Canada. I am praying that the Lord will give me a permanent teammate-companion-secretary who is willing to dedicate her life one hundred percent to the Lord's work. My, she must have so many qualities to be fitted for this work that I sometimes think I am praying for what is called in Holland "a sheep with five legs" [the impossible]. But the Lord knows the right person and the right time: I wait upon Him.

To Australasia with Revival Fellowship

Early in 1956 Corrie was invited by Dr. J. Edwin Orr to take part in revival meetings in Australasia as part of his Revival Fellowship Team. He was an authority in the study of revival, and Tante Corrie called his books on this subject "a great contribution to the story of the evangelical Church." She had the utmost respect for him and frequently referred to him and his work.

In June 1957 she wrote:

Australia is not an easy country to work in, but God blesses the efforts of the Revival Team with whom I work. Sometimes we work together as a team in one place but often spread out over several suburbs and hold campaigns of one or two weeks' duration in each. We do not yet see revival but know that the Holy Spirit works in the hearts of many Christians, and prayer groups are formed to pray for revival. Our schedule is full. Three meetings a day is the regular program, and often there is no free day between the campaigns.

But we work for a General who has never lost a battle, so it is worthwhile to give our one hundred percent. Will you please pray for us for wisdom to arrange skillfully and for strength from on high for our spirits, minds and bodies?

Not long after this Tante Corrie headed to New Zealand. From there she wrote:

Mrs. McKenzie, a dear saint in Otorohanga, had heard me in Auckland and organized a campaign in her own town. She wrote me: "Corrie, I love you already for the happy message you bring. I will take good care of you and not give you too many meetings. But there is a crippled girl in a hospital I will visit with you. She is very near to the valley of the shadow of death but hopes to meet you before she dies."

That same day Mrs. McKenzie herself died suddenly. I did not know the name of the crippled girl she had wanted me to visit. I prayed that the Lord would guide me to her, and I found her. Poor little Grace. She was a dwarf with hands out of place. I never saw such a poor body. But her soul was radiant because she was filled with the Holy Spirit. I could not understand everything she said—her voice was very weak—but I understood that she said, "Go to my mother, please, and bring her to the Lord." We prayed together for her, and that same day I had the joy of bringing the mother to the great decision for Jesus Christ. When Grace heard it she said, "Now I can die." Two days later she died.

Also during her time with Revival Fellowship Corrie met a special young man:

While in Melbourne I met a Dutchman from my own hometown of Haarlem, who asked me, "Do you remember that thirteen years ago you sent me a Jewish baby of two weeks old?"

"No," I answered, "I only remember that there were a hundred babies from a Jewish Orphanage and that we distributed them to a hundred families, but I really do not remember to whom I sent them."

"Well, here is one of them," he answered, and before me stood Martin, a lovely boy. He looked with interest at the Dutch lady who had saved his life thirteen years before. A bit later I had the great joy of bringing him to a decision for the Lord Jesus.

Next day in school he gave his first testimony, "Boys," he said, "yesterday I met the lady who saved my life when I was two weeks old, and boys, listen. I think I will be a good boy now, for she has told me how to ask Jesus to come into my heart, and He will make me good."

And also from Australia Corrie wrote about her love for prison ministry:

In a women's prison I gave an invitation to accept the Lord Jesus. One woman came to the Lord, and she told me, "I have been sentenced to two weeks in jail. I know why I had to be here, for I found here my Savior Jesus Christ." *Work in prisons is still the work that has my heart more than any other.*

In November 1957, Corrie's work with Revival Fellowship came to a close. "After two years in Australasia, I am now called to India, Borneo, Korea, Japan and wherever the Lord leads me."

Water Baptism

On March 20, 1958, Corrie was baptized by immersion in the William Carey Baptist Church in Calcutta by Walter G. Corbett. Later she was to tell about it:

I was re-baptized in a small Baptist church in India. In the morning I spoke to Baptists about baptism in the morning service. In the afternoon I was baptized again by immersion. I think baptism by immersion is Biblical—fuller than by sprinkling. This baptism is a better symbol of being "buried with Christ" by going under the water and then rising up with Him out of the water purified.

A Discovery of God's Provision

Finally in 1959, at the end of this decade, fifteen years after her release from concentration camp, Corrie was part of a group that revisited Ravensbrück to honor Betsie and the thousands of other women who had died there. Checking the records, she discovered that her own release had been the result of a clerical error. A week after she was released all women her age died in the gas chamber.

nine

Lessons from Argentina and Africa

1960–1963

In 1960 Corrie received the answer to her prayer for a permanent traveling companion. The solitary life had never become easy for the pronounced extrovert. I remember her saying to me when I joined her in 1976, "At the beginning of my travels around the world I went on a journey that lasted six years. Soon after that came another world journey that took six years. Then the Lord gave me Conny, who was with me for seven years, then Ellen, who was with me for nearly nine years, and now I have you."

Conny

Here is how Corrie described the gifted first companion God gave her: "The Lord saw and supplied my need in the person of Conny van Hoogstraten, a beautiful, young Dutch woman. ... I met her on one of my visits to England, where she was attending a Bible school. We laughed much together, for the

Lord had given her an infectious sense of humor and a happy laughter."

Corrie and Conny were to undertake extensive work journeys together between 1960 and 1967. Corrie said of her companion, "We really do three times as much work than I did when I was alone."

In May and June 1961 Corrie wrote about one of her early travels with Conny:

> I am now sitting in the midst of a palm wood in Kerala State. The wind makes a beautiful music with the waving palm leaves. The weather is hot. Often I pray, "Lord, be my coolness!" And He is.
>
> Three months in India—what an experience! This country of millions of people gives such an opportunity to reach Christians and to show them the victorious life, and to tell sinners the way of salvation through Jesus. Conny reaches often the children. She arranges meetings for them in the time that I reach the grownups. Sometimes it happens that first the children come to the Lord and after that the parents come. A man told me that he was so happy that his little son had accepted the Lord Jesus. He wanted to do the same but was not able. I found out that he had fallen into witchcraft-sin. I read Deuteronomy 18:10–13 with him, and he confessed. But only after we had cast out the demons was he free to receive the Lord Jesus as his personal Savior. How we need wisdom and strength from on high. Without Jesus we can do nothing, nothing—with Him much, very much" [see John 15:5].

Lessons from Africa

Leaving India and going on to Africa, Corrie wrote to her friends about some of the most important lessons that helped her lead a victorious life:

147

Living for the Moment

Dear Friends,

The Lord gives me always the grace to live in the present, not in the future or past. In India I thought, "In this country is the most important work I ever had to do. How I love the Indians!" Now I am in Africa, and I can say the same. Africa is the most inspiring surrounding. Such openness and hunger for the messages I did not see elsewhere, and I surely can add—How I love the Africans!

The Answer for Problems of the Heart

The eight months Conny and Corrie spent in Africa from April to December of 1961 were particularly significant:

This year from April until December we traveled in active service from Ethiopia to Cape Town, working in eight countries. All the time I was conscious of the fact that I was in the midst of political tensions. It has made me still more thankful that God has called us here, for the root of all the controversies is sin, and Jesus is the answer.

To me the climax was again when I could speak in prisons. I wish that more Christian men and women felt the call to work in prisons and reformatories. We know the answer for the problems in the heart of every decent or indecent sinner. Jesus says to all, "Come to me, and I will give you rest." And how very precious is every soul in His loving eyes.

Walking in the Light

When Corrie and Conny arrived in East Africa for the first time in 1961, the famous East Africa Revival had already been taking place for many years. Its distinguishing mark was that Christians took very seriously the importance of "walking in the light with each other," following the New Testament's instruction: "If we walk in the light, as He is in the light, we have fellowship with one another, and the blood of Jesus His Son purifies us from every sin" (see 1 John 1:7). As soon as East African Christians found themselves out of fellowship with another, they became strongly convicted to confess their sin and ask forgiveness of each other and the Lord. Having been cleansed from sin with fellowship restored, they could experience victorious life. If Christians failed to reconcile with each other, it could be that the Lord would not answer their prayers for growth and continued revival.

I was to see "walking in the light" in action myself when I lived and worked in East Africa in the mid-1960s. Its practice is undoubtedly a big reason for the ongoing revival. Tante Corrie found it such an important lesson that she taught it for the rest of her life. And she definitely lived it—in the first place with Conny!

Every day I am more thankful that God gave me my "Timothy," my co-pilot and co-everything. We live "in the light" as soon as the enemy tries to attack the personal relationship between us, that strategic point for many missionaries. We repent together and to each other. I am an old veteran, hardened in the battle, and especially during those terrible months in the concentration camp I learned not to mind little hardships. As a "tramp for the Lord" I have lived in more than a thousand homes during the last fifteen years. [Conny] has still to get used to this life, and to learn that her sufficiency is of the Lord in all circumstances of life. I believe that it is one of the secrets of a happy Christian's life: to draw on the Unfailing Source—Jesus Christ—for every situation and every new adjustment we have to make. But the Lord gives us much grace, and we praise Him for giving us this work to do together. We both enjoy life.

The Sin of Worry

In her thousands of messages, Corrie often taught about the sin of worry. Nancy, one of her hostesses during that long journey through Africa in 1961, later wrote about this lesson that Corrie taught her:

> She was sitting in the front seat beside me in my old car, and I asked her, "Corrie, what is your secret? How do you live in the light?" As I spoke, the windshield wiper squeaked slightly as it cleared away the heavy raindrops of a sudden shower.
>
> "That is the secret," Corrie said, pointing to the moving windshield wiper. "It is the little decent sins—things like worry and unforgiveness—that cloud our spiritual vision. Don't wait until nightfall, Nancy. You started the wiper as soon as you could not see clearly."
>
> "But, Corrie, worry isn't a sin."
>
> "Oh, yes, it is, Nancy. Worry is a sin. If you are worrying you are not trusting God. Not to trust God is a sin."
>
> But still I pressed her, "You cannot tell me that things like impatience and irritability are really sins. These are character defects."
>
> "They *are* sins," she interrupted, "and there is no verse in the Bible that says God forgives excuses. You will never grow if you bring God only excuses."

Removing Rags in Argentina

Early in 1962, shortly after their eight months' stay in Africa, Corrie and Conny spent a month in Argentina. Her letter to her friends gives us another clear lesson from her life—how she quickly turned to the Lord, instead of complaining when plans seemed to have gone wrong.

> This was the first time God called us to go to this country. After forty hours of traveling by jet plane from Entebbe, Uganda, we arrived in Buenos Aires. It is always a thrill to be called to a new country, and we were looking forward to the blessings the Lord had in store for us.

The minister who met us at the airport asked us [if] we had not received his letter. He had written us that it was perhaps better not to come at this time to Argentina since it was holiday time. The key people were out of town, and no meetings could be arranged. After our talk I asked myself why the Lord had sent us here, but I trusted Him, for He never makes a mistake.

The first meeting I had was some hours' traveling away, and then I could speak for twenty ladies. The enemy told me that it was all wrong to go to this little church, since I am so used to speaking for large congregations. But then I repented of my pride. How often we forget that we are "nobodies," just gloves who cannot do anything by themselves. It is the Hand in the glove who is able. "Without Me you can do nothing," Jesus says [see John 15:5].

And now, after having been in Argentina for a month, I can tell about unusual blessings. Dr. Gwen Shepherd, a children's doctor and specialist for polio cases, gave me her furnished flat to live in, and I enjoyed it very much to be for a whole month in the same rooms. And God opened doors and hearts. Students, doctors, prisoners and Jews were reached.

Dr. Shepherd reported on Corrie's visit some years later:

For four weeks I translated Corrie's message into Spanish. One morning I came to the flat and found Corrie sitting on the blue divan tearing up a piece of cloth and stuffing the strips into her flashlight.

"Corrie, what on earth are you doing?"

"Preparing my props," she answered with a twinkle in her eye.

"Props?"

"Yes, props for my talks. Sometimes university students object to visual aids, but I find that even intellectuals sometimes need practical illustrations in order to understand my message. Everyone can see that a flashlight cannot shine if it is full of rags." I was soon to see the effect of her "props."

"Gwen, have you ever been in a prison?"

"No, Corrie, I have not."

"Would you like to visit one?"

"Can't say I am especially keen."

But, keen or not, Corrie and I were flown in a small army plane halfway across the country as VIP visitors to the model prison at Santa Rosa de la Pampas, where she was invited to speak to the men.

"Men," she said, "I know what it is like to be behind bars and to be shut up in solitary confinement."

How they listened—a hall full of tidily dressed prisoners, with the Governor, his wife and little daughter and the rest of the prison authorities in the front row. They heard Corrie tell about God's love for each one of them and how life could be wonderful even behind bars, if they walked in His light. Out came her flashlight. A school-boyish sniggering swept over the hall as she vainly tried to click it—a reaction that quickly turned to a hushed silence as one by one the rags of sin were pulled out of it.

A few months later, shortly after her seventieth birthday, April 15, 1962, Corrie wrote to her prayer partners:

This morning I prayed again that I may decrease and that Jesus may increase. Then I received a letter from the mayor of my hometown, Haarlem, Holland, in which he wrote that it has pleased Her Majesty the Queen to give me the decoration of Knight in the Order of Orange Nassau. When I read that letter I fear that a little rag came into my flashlight. It was the sin of pride, but I brought it to the Lord. He forgave and cleansed me with His blood, and now I just accept this honor from the hand of the Lord and my Queen with great thankfulness.

Will you pray that more and more people in the meetings may see Jesus and that I may be hidden behind the cross?

Ever the Learner

After her Argentinean adventures, Corrie and Conny traveled to the United States of America. During Billy Graham's crusade in Chicago in 1962 they signed on as two of the many counselors who at the end of each evening would counsel those who responded to Graham's invitation to accept the Lord Jesus Christ. Although she had brought the Gospel to others since her childhood, she was ever the learner:

> Our days are so full and blessed, and I had a great experience to be in Chicago and join the campaign of Billy Graham. Conny and I both studied the training course for counselors, and like the other 4,000 counselors we worked as much as possible after the meetings in the inquiry rooms. We learned much, also for the future. To counsel standing in the midst of hundreds of people embarrassed me sometimes. I am sure I made many mistakes. But what joy it was to see people coming to a first decision for Jesus Christ, or to a new surrender.

Years later Corrie herself would be invited to give her testimony from crusade platforms.

And during that same time in 1962, Corrie wrote something that showed how she continually let her Lord teach her as well:

> On one occasion I was very cross with the important gentleman who had arranged my program. Everything was very badly organized, not because of incapability but through sheer carelessness. After the meeting I told him what I thought of him in no uncertain terms. He looked rather astounded but did not say a word.
>
> However, that night God had a word with me. I rang the gentleman up the next morning and apologized.
>
> "Oh, that's okay," he answered, "I told my wife about the dressing-down I had received last night and how I felt

like a guilty schoolboy being reprimanded by the teacher. But I also told her that I really deserved it, so please don't apologize."

"But," I said to him, "I do owe you an apology. What I said to you was right, but not the way I said it!"

A Movie?

Several times during the decade of the sixties, Corrie asked her friends and prayer partners to pray that her book *A Prisoner and Yet* . . . would become a motion picture. At the time of the Cuban missile crisis of 1962 she wrote:

Some weeks ago two American Christians met to discuss the possibilities of what they could do for their country. They both knew that in the USA much is being done to fight communism by organizations such as the Christian Anti-Communist League, which by means of literature and the spoken word informs the public about the nature and aim of communism. These men asked each other: "Is it necessary that we, too, use our time to fight communism? Is it not very necessary to show people that when the worst happens in the life of a Christian the best remains? Jesus is not limited in giving His strength and comfort in times of hardship."

The next day these two men heard about the possibility of making a film of my book, *A Prisoner and Yet.* . . . They saw this as an answer to their questions. In that book God gave me grace to show that in my life Jesus' light was stronger than the deepest darkness of the concentration camp. Now these men will do their best to have this book filmed.

Will you pray for that enterprise? Pray that good actors may be found and that the words of the Gospel may be spoken by people who stand behind the message with their faith and life. It is possible that this film will be used to bring the Gospel in places where it never has been heard before.

Corrie's faith and prayers would be rewarded in the coming decade when John and Elizabeth Sherrill developed and enlarged on the story in *A Prisoner and Yet* . . . The book *The Hiding Place* would be published in 1971. And in 1975, the movie of the same name would be released by World Wide Pictures, the filmmaking arm of the Billy Graham Evangelistic Association.

ten

When Bad Things Happen

1963–1968

The year 1963 would take Corrie and Conny to several places around the world. Each one offered unique ways for Corrie to share her message before she headed home to Holland for a forced rest.

A Retreat Center in Uganda

It was God's plan that Corrie spend more time in Africa as the 1960s unfolded. She wrote to her friends early in 1963:

Since a long time, some of my friends and I have prayed for people, a house and money to open an interracial, international and interdenominational center where races can find each other at the foot of the cross of Jesus Christ. We did not know where the Lord was intending to give us this center—Holland, Switzerland, Israel, Australia? A place where we can have conferences to train young people and where people can come for retreats and for rest.

In Uganda God brought me in contact with Christians who had the same vision. God gave there a house with a beautiful garden around it. In Uganda, East Africa, between Entebbe and Kampala lies Lweza. Men who have been mightily used in the continuous revival in Africa and over a big part of the world have joined hands, and so we are now in the process of rebuilding the house. An open-air church, guest rooms and cottages for workers and many more plans will come into being there, the Lord willing.

She then listed the men whom God so greatly used—members with her on the planning committee: Dr. J. E. Church, Mr. Festo Kivengere, Mr. William Nagenda, Bishop Eric Sabiti of the Anglican Church in Uganda, and Mr. Harry Campbell.

Argentina, Brazil and Holland

On July 8, 1963, Corrie wrote to Bobbie Halliday: "We are now in the jungle in northeast Argentina. A revival started in a church. Christians started to live in the light. Sinners were saved. Hallelujah. . . . We are now leaving for Brazil."

And two months later, from Holland to her friends:

This letter I have written partly in South America, partly in Holland. "Knocked down, but not knocked out." I had to leave South America because my health gave in. I had an infection of the liver. Now I am in Holland, and when the Lord has healed me, I hope to take a time of rest and finish a book that I began to write. The Lord has made it clear to me that I had not taken sufficient rest between the campaigns, so I think it is His discipline to bring me alone with Him for a while. Will you pray for perfect healing? It was a very sad thing to have to cancel all the appointments for the rest of the year.

After five weeks of illness, of which I spent two in the hospital, I am completely healthy again. The Lord is guiding me to stay in Holland until the end of the year to spend much time alone with Him.

To Germany

In July 1964 Corrie was back in Germany. She wrote:

Oh, it is such a joy that the Lord uses me this time in Germany for many prisoners! But also for ministers. More than before, I am involved in their congresses and meetings.

The ministers and I got along well, working, praying and striving together. Although we differed in background and training, our common aim united us: the winning of souls for eternity and helping the children of God to learn that "Jesus is Victor."

Speaking at a ministers' meeting is another story. Frequently it was among them that I found my severest critics, and sometimes even my greatest opposition. Yet it seemed vital to be used by God among them, for these men who worked in over-large congregations and were weighed down with problems also needed to be reminded of Jesus' victory and His plan for the world.

A large group waited for me to speak. Should I try to convince them not to listen to me but to God and His message for us?

"Gentlemen, I am a lay person, a lay woman, a Dutch lay woman. Are there some present who would rather not remain?

"I intend to speak about conversion. Perhaps you have a label for me—a pietist? I shall talk about the Lord's return—that should label me a sectarian. I may even speak about the rapture of the Church—that makes me a fanatic. Or the fullness of the Holy Spirit—a Pentecostal. Keep your labels handy, gentlemen. Should my words touch your consciences, you have only to label me, set me in a corner and have nothing to fear."

A strange thing happened. The critical faces relaxed. There was laughter, after which we truly listened together to God's message: Germany's great need, and Christ the answer to this need. The world's history is a great embroidery by God, enough of which is made clear to us through His Word so that we can face the future calmly and securely since all is in His hand. Indeed, the best is yet to be—a world full of the knowledge of the Lord, as the waters cover the sea.

When I finished, with one accord the group turned to prayer.[1]

The following she wrote to her friends concerning Germany in that same letter of 1964:

When I spoke about our wonderful commission, given to us by the Lord in Mark 16:15–18, one minister said to me, "I know that there are people in my parish who are possessed. But is it my task to cast out the demons?" Then I answered, "Who else should do it? We who have the name of Jesus are the only ones who have this authority." Another minister said, "But how does one know whether it is a case of demons or of mental illness?" I answered, "Here we may take the promise given in James 1:5. All wisdom we need is given to us in this verse. We need only to cash the check."

The Gifts of the Holy Spirit

I am so happy that lately many people's eyes are being opened for the gifts of the Holy Spirit, in Germany as well as in

South America and many other countries of the world. I am convinced that the Lord will fulfill the promises of Joel 2:28, even in the main denominations. The whole atmosphere is changing. I believe that the Lord will do great things. When a person is open for the Lord Jesus Christ and all that He wants to give, and is closed to the world and all that the world wants to give, he is levelheaded. Here in Germany many people are still afraid of fanatics and excesses, but when we take the promises of 1 Corinthians 14:12 seriously and covet the best gifts earnestly (see 1 Corinthians 12:31), we have nothing to fear and God will do miracles. How unbiblical is the assertion that we need only to love and that the gifts of the Spirit are superfluous. On the contrary! Paul begins 1 Corinthians 14 with the twofold sentence: "Follow the way of love, *and* earnestly (eagerly) desire spiritual gifts."

Still writing from Germany in the summer of 1964, Corrie says:

During a meeting in East Berlin I received flowers from a group of young people from the town of Ravensbrück with the request that I come and speak in the church. We could arrange it with our program, and so it happened that we had a meeting in the old church at the border of the lovely little lake that I had seen when, tortured by thirst, I entered the concentration camp about twenty years ago. Betsie and I suffered so much there, but now I could tell here how I had come through alive and victorious, not through my faith, which was weak and wavering, but carried by Jesus Himself. Jesus, who is willing to sustain everyone who is in need and willing to surrender his or her life into His strong and never failing hands.

How wonderful is God's plan with my life! First a struggle with death in a terrible prison, and now I can bring in the same place the Word of Life to free people.

A Sabbatical

Near the end of this same year, Corrie was diagnosed with hepatitis. She was now 72 years old and had been traveling for seventeen years without any long break.

The doctor has advised me to rest for some time, and the Lord has shown me that I must take a sabbatical year. No wheels of cars, trains and airplanes beneath me. Alone with the Lord and with Conny, I hope to receive new inspiration and strength and to be able to write.

Corrie was to spend most of her sabbatical year at Lweza, Uganda, East Africa, in housing provided for her and Conny at the beautiful conference center that had come into being partly through her own prayers and work. Before she left, however, she spent almost two months at the house of a German doctor:

Never before have I had a medical treatment like during that time. There was so much prayer and care. God blessed that treatment, and now I am healthy again and can enjoy the sabbatical year. There are no meetings, no traveling, but I am walking, resting, studying and listening to the Lord. What a privilege!

But Corrie, who disliked rest in terms of it being the opposite of work, also found the prospect of a sabbatical daunting:

Sometimes I regret that I cannot and may not travel and have meetings during this sabbatical year. I know God can use only obedient servants, and He has made it so clear that I must take this time of rest. I experience that just in the moments when I regret this time of different activity, the Lord always arranges it so I receive an encouraging letter to show me that the work is going on and the seed is sprouting out.

One of the secrets of Corrie's victorious life was that she carried out her work from a position of rest in the Lord. She absolutely loved work. To her it had nothing to do with personal attainment. It was obedience. In March 1965 she wrote:

> We have arrived in the little paradise of Lweza. From a cold winter in Europe to a heat wave in a country very near the equator. For six months there had been no rain at all, but yesterday it rained, and it is as if the flowers and trees are smiling with joy. We enjoy the singing of the birds and the stillness of the tropical nights, but most of all we rejoice because of the fellowship with the Christians here.
>
> I am still recharging my spiritual and physical batteries by reading the Bible, listening to the Lord and resting on an easy chair in this beautiful garden. Two nice dogs are lying at my feet. When I look to the right I see Lake Victoria in the distance. Crickets are chirping. A kind African brings me an extra pillow. The whole atmosphere is full of beauty and peace. It is a miracle how much one can do even during such a time of rest—correspondence, writing articles, revising a manuscript for a book, intercession and being quiet to listen to the Lord so that He will recharge our spiritual batteries.

Corrie's sabbatical year also included work with Conny in prisons, hospitals, schools and churches.

When Corrie started her sabbatical year at the end of 1964 she told her friends: "I asked the Lord that after this year of rest, if He has not returned, to give me another ten years of work with new strength and inspiration." The Lord gave her more than that.

And when her rest year came to a close in the autumn of 1965 she wrote: "There is great joy in my heart to begin again. The Lord willing, first in Africa, then in Aden and Israel, then perhaps for a short time in the U.S.A. and Canada and then in

Eastern Europe, where we hope that the Lord will open doors in countries we did not reach until now."

Following the Sabbatical

Before she left the African continent, Corrie was to work in several countries there, including Kenya, Tanzania, Ethiopia and the Congo. She also revisited two small countries south of Uganda—Rwanda and Burundi. On an earlier visit she had been deeply affected by the tribal warfare in Rwanda and Burundi in which hundreds of thousands of people, many of them Christians, lost their lives very brutally. Her own experiences of suffering gave her unusual authority to comfort.

> Once I spoke for about one thousand people in Rwanda. Many of them had burnt the houses of their enemies, and there were also the people whose houses were burnt. To speak to such people about the miracle that when Jesus tells us to love our enemies He will Himself give us the love He demands from us is a timely message. I could tell them about my problem. I had had hatred for the murderers of my family, but I brought that hatred to the Lord, and He forgave and cleansed me and sometimes even used me to bring my former enemies to Him. Those people there in Rwanda understood that what I told was not theory or theology but real experience.

The Greatest Joy for a Christian

Corrie had heard many Christians speak of the annual Keswick conferences for Christian growth in England. In the autumn of 1965 another appointment at the end of her sabbatical year was in Nairobi, Kenya, where she was a speaker at the East Africa Keswick Convention.

The Lord gave me to speak about the joy of total surrender. I mentioned the "if onlys" and told about my "if only I was married," which I had when I was young. The boy whom I loved chose another girl, and I surrendered that "if only" to the Lord Jesus to whom I belonged. It was a short battle, and then victory and peace came. The miracle happened that this "creative" part of a woman's life that she needs for marriage life and having children, the Lord used in His Kingdom. I never had the joy to bring a child to birth, but often God used me to bring someone to rebirth—and that is the greatest joy for a Christian. The Lord undertook and gave me a very happy life so that I never became a "frustrated old spinster."

It was the year after this that I arrived to work in Nairobi, Kenya, and heard Corrie's name for the first time at that momentous prayer meeting I described in chapter 1: "I would like to ask prayer for Corrie ten Boom," the lady in the floral dress at the front of the room had said. "She is in her midseventies now and has recently spent many months in Uganda. Her doctor had prescribed a sabbatical rest for her. But now she has resumed her world journeys." I had already made my own surrender to the Lord, the biggest of which was the laying down of the right to marriage. It would be ten years before I joined Tante Corrie in her work. I can confirm that she certainly was not a frustrated old spinster, and her example of the joyful acceptance of her singleness as part of God's plan was greatly encouraging to me.

A New Home in Holland

In the summer of 1966 the work she had started in Bloemendaal twenty years earlier became exclusively a rehabilitation home for Dutch people who needed rest and medical care. Corrie's work there ended rather abruptly and sadly. She seldom referred to her parting of the ways with those who helped her make reality of

Betsie's first vision, but years later, when she lived in California, she explained to me what happened.

At the time though, she wrote to her friends simply this: "Soon I hope to be able to give you my new address where Conny and I will have a home and an office, where we will live during the few days that we are from time to time in Holland."

Indeed a good home was provided. A Dutch baroness who spent most of her time working in Israel gave Corrie the use of her beautiful apartment in Soestdijk near the royal palace. It was to be her base for some years.

A New Teammate

Corrie's 75th birthday, April 15, 1967, was spent working with her old friend Brother Andrew in Vietnam. And in September of that year, Conny married Lykle Hoogerzeil, a Dutch missionary doctor to India.

During the weeks before Conny's marriage a day came when she was sure they had found the right person to take her place as Corrie's companion. It was the day that tall, blonde Ellen de Kroon came to meet with them about the unusual vacancy needing to be filled. Among other things, Conny noticed the loving way in which Ellen, thinking that Tante Corrie might be a little cold, found a blanket and tucked her into it as she sat in her chair. Again, God provided for Corrie. She wrote:

> The Lord gave me another helper, Ellen de Kroon. She has been a nurse but has surrendered herself to this quite new work of being my teammate. We appreciate your prayers for her. We are having lots of fun already, and it is a real challenge for her to start such an adventurous life of dependence on the Lord.
>
> Conny and Lykle are now in Utrecht preparing for the mission field. What joy it has been to have Conny during seven years as my fellow tramp for the Lord. Not only what she did, but also what she was has been such a blessing for

the work and for me. She herself is so thankful to the Lord for the time of preparation for the mission field these seven years gave her, with all the work in God's Kingdom all over the world together with me, as a team, side by side.

During the months that Conny and Lykle were preparing to leave for India, Corrie was happy that they lived nearby. They visited her often, and Conny and Ellen also had the opportunity to discuss what living and working with Tante Corrie involved. When time allowed, Conny was able to help Corrie now and then.

An Accident

Late in 1967 Corrie was involved in a serious car accident while on her way to record some messages in Dutch for her friends at Trans World Radio. She wrote to her friends:

For Trans World Radio I often give short messages in the Dutch language that reach many people who understand our language over all the world. This time I was asked to give a talk about our victory over demons. The Lord gave me three strong messages. The title of the first was *Are We Powerless Against Demons? No!* And I told about the authority of the name of Jesus and the power of His blood. We overcome by the blood of the Lamb and by the power the Holy Spirit gives us.

On the day that I [was to] give these messages over the radio, I got involved in a rather serious car accident. Conny, who was driving, was not injured. By a miracle both our lives were spared. The little combs in my hair were broken in pieces. So my head could have been severely wounded, but only my right arm was broken in four places. During the accident I could only cry, "Jesus, Jesus."

When I was lying in the hospital with my broken arm, I thought about what had happened and I understood that it was very well possible that the enemy did not like those messages about the Christian's victory over the devil. So he tried to get me knocked out. He really has got me knocked down, but the Lord has spared my life. But I had to stay in hospital for two months and suffered very much pain.

I also saw that this experience was a little bit of cross-bearing. When Jesus died on the cross, He destroyed Satan's head. In the Old Testament the promise was given: "The LORD God said to the serpent . . . I will put enmity between you and the woman, and between your offspring and hers; he will crush your head" (Genesis 3:14–15).

In the New Testament, Paul says, "By His death He (Jesus) might destroy him who holds the power of death, that is, the devil" (Hebrews 2:14). My radio messages were meant to show the Christians this victory over demons through Jesus. That is why I saw it as cross-bearing, too. Then I said to the Lord: "You have suffered terrible pain at the cross in your great love. Your pains and love were mixed together. Will you now make me to experience Romans 5:5? You have poured out your love into my heart by the Holy Spirit. Please mix your love with my pain." When I had prayed this prayer, I could bear the suffering.

I learned much in this time. It was one of the difficult classes of my life. But again Jesus stood in front of the class. I can praise His name.

The Foolishness of God

"Her life hung by a silken thread," said Hans van der Steen, the director of Trans World Radio in Holland, speaking of the time after the accident. He and Corrie were good friends, having first met in the late 1940s when Corrie returned from her first journey to the United States, full of zeal and new knowledge about how to spread the Gospel. She was very interested in Trans World Radio, and during her short times in Holland between her travels Hans recorded her messages for broadcast. One day they were having an animated conversation about how the radio work in Holland began and the wonderful things God did as a result of it.

"Stop for a minute," said Corrie. She walked out of the room, stood at the bottom of the stairs and called loudly, "Conny, come down quickly. Come and listen to the foolishness of God."

Corrie liked using that expression, and she liked teaching on the subject.

How we need to have good vision in this time when all is so dark. The Holy Spirit gives us good eyes that we may see God's plan in the midst of all the chaos of this time. In 1 Corinthians 1 and 2 we read about the "foolishness" of God and the "wisdom of the wise." Two realms they are: The wisdom of the wise is all we can grasp with our logical thinking, with our brains; the foolishness of God, the greatest wisdom, we can touch only with our faith knowledge. The Holy Spirit teaches us to lift up the wisdom of the wise to the height of the foolishness of God, and then we get the vision. When people do not know the Lord and are not born into the family of God, they cannot see and they cannot understand the Kingdom of God, because they have only their logical thinking, the use of their brains. And when you try to bring the foolishness of God under the criticism of the wisdom of the wise, then you may end up with a theology that says, "God is dead."

We live in a period [in which] one of the signs of the end time [that] Daniel gave becomes very clear: "Knowledge shall be increased" (Daniel 12:4, KJV). Some people expect that in the coming ten years the sum total of human knowledge will be doubled. [She wrote this in 1968.]

It is such a great danger when only our logical thinking gives us guidance. It may become a real weapon in the hands of the antichrist. I experienced that personally at a congress of communists in Ravensbrück. I heard that a reunion of ex-prisoners was to be held, and I hoped to find friends with whom I had suffered. Instead, forty thousand communists were present. I listened to their talks, and such darkness fell upon me that when I returned to West Germany I had the feeling that I had no message at all. Then people prayed with me, and the Lord liberated me totally, and I received a strong message from Him. But there I saw how dangerous it is to be permanently in the atmosphere of the wisdom of the wise without any knowledge of the foolishness of God, which is the highest wisdom.

The wisdom of the wise is not something that is wrong in itself. We belong to the Lord one hundred percent with heart and mind. And when we have surrendered both to Him, He will show us how to use that wisdom. I remember that when I was a watchmaker with my old father, he once said, "My name is on the shop, but really God's name should be on the shop, because I am a watchmaker by the grace of God." Sometimes we could not find what was wrong with a watch and then we prayed that the Lord would show it to us. And Father and I, we both had the joyful experience that in our dreams in the night the Lord showed us the fault in the watch. When it happened with me, I went down to the workshop and looked [to see] if my dream was true. Always I found the answer to the problem. Yes, there is nothing too great for God's power; there is nothing too small for His love.

The Right Side of the Embroidery

Corrie was very intelligent, but she was not an intellectual. On matters of suffering she was distressed but did not question God. She learned to ask God to show her a little bit of His side of the embroidery of her life.

I mentioned earlier that after her imprisonment she asked God to let her see her suffering "just a little bit from your point of view." God answered and Corrie obeyed. The lives of countless people were changed as she taught them that the Lord Jesus was able to turn loss into glory. When I worked with Corrie she frequently asked Him to show her things "more and more from Your point of view."

And she surely made that same prayer when Conny was diagnosed with a malignancy. Conny was never able to accompany her husband to the mission field because she became very seriously ill.

Conny was to pass away in 1970. It was then that Corrie wrote about the end of Conny's life:

> Her illness became worse and she was in the hospital, finding it hard to breathe because of fluid on her lungs. When I got to her room she said, "Take an easy chair." She showed concern for the needs of others, was kind to the people around her and had no trace of self-pity. It was as if she did not know how to play the role of a critically ill person. She talked a lot about what she had read in her Bible.
>
> Once she said, "Tante Corrie, I often thought I would have to bury you, and now you have to do that for me."
>
> God does not make mistakes. We cannot understand His ways, but Conny already knows the answer. God has shown her His side of the embroidery of her life—the upper side—while we still see the wrong side—the underside.
>
> At Conny's funeral I prayed: "Thank You, Father, in Jesus' name that Conny is now with You. Would You make us all ready to come into Your presence? Her work on earth is finished. Use us, make us faithful, to keep burning the lights which have been lit by her in Your strength. Fill us, therefore, with Your Holy Spirit. Make us also faithful unto death, so that we will receive the crown of life. Amen."

eleven

Extraordinary Years, Extraordinary Results

1968–1976

llen de Kroon and Corrie became close and effective co-workers for nearly nine years. Ellen's nursing ability must have been of great comfort to Corrie after the serious car accident and at many other times as she approached and entered her eighties. Ellen had a good sense of humor and love for people. In their first years together they traveled to Germany, Israel, England, Russia, Switzerland, France, Cuba, Mexico, Kazakhstan, Tajikistan, Uzbekistan, Cyprus and the United States, among other countries.

Ellen was to accompany Corrie through some of the most extraordinary years of her life—years in which a book and movie would make her message available to millions. But there were other significant events in which Ellen had the privilege to share.

Yad Vashem

One of the first foreign journeys Ellen and Corrie made together was to Israel. On February 28, 1968, the 24th anniversary of their arrest at the Beje, Corrie and her deceased relatives were honored by the state of Israel.

Corrie described this as a very moving experience in which she and a Dutch couple were honored. The ceremony took place in Jerusalem at Yad Vashem, a memorial and museum built in memory of the martyrs and heroes of World War II. Corrie wrote:

Heroes are considered those who gave themselves to save Jewish people during the war. The staff of Yad Vashem invited me to come to them to give them the opportunity to honor my family and me. When I arrived, a large crowd was already present. Together with the Dutch couple I stood in the center of the big hall where they would honor us. First a rabbi chanted a litany in memory of the dead. The voices of Jews are so beautiful; they can express sadness and suffering in such a moving way. This rabbi sang in memory of those members of my family who died for the Jews. It was so intensely sad and moving. While he sang, however, birds came all the time, singing their happy song as a joyful background, an accompaniment to the chant for the dead.

There was a litany in memory of the dead, a child read a psalm and speeches were made. This was followed by a visit outside to the "Avenue of the Righteous" where I planted a tree (with my healed arm, praise the Lord). Here every tree has a small plaque at its base bearing the name of the "Righteous Gentile" who planted it.

But to Corrie the most important thing was the opportunity to thank those who had given such a high honor to her and her family for their part in saving Jewish people. "What an opportunity the Lord gave me to bring the Gospel to many Jews in an official position who were present, just by simply telling about my family."

The Death of a Friend

In 1969 Corrie received news of the death of the Christian leader Abraham Vereide, one of her earliest friends in America. You will recall that when no doors opened for Corrie on her first visit to the States in 1946, it was he who wrote letters and made telephone calls on her behalf. Soon she had more invitations than she could accept.

Corrie wrote:

> Abraham Vereide went from his work to be with the Lord. He had traveled that week to speak at several breakfast groups. He read at the dinner table a word from the Bible and prayed. Then he said, "I am so very, very happy today. It is as if I have got a new baptism of the Holy Spirit." Some hours later he was with the Lord. No sickness, no suffering. He really died in the harness at 82 years old.

Tante Corrie longed that she might die "in the harness," too. She often told me that she wanted to go straight "from service good, to service best." I believe the Lord gave her that desire, but not in the way she would have chosen.

On Dutch Television

In 1971 Corrie received an unusual invitation that brought her much joy: the opportunity to appear as a guest on a very popular secular Dutch television program. Many people in the Netherlands had never shown interest in her story—a prophetess is without honor in her own country—but now she was asked by TV personality Willem Duys to tell about her trips around the world and to give a short Easter message:

> Because it was not a Christian television program, I reached many people who were not expecting to hear such a mes-

173

sage—perhaps six million people, I was told [nearly half of the population of Holland at the time]. The results were tremendous. Letters, phone calls and visits made the next weeks full of important work for Ellen and me. Many people who needed spiritual help came for counseling. Doors and hearts opened in churches and groups. Many found the Lord Jesus. People who had seen me on the TV invited me to come to various cities. And many people with whom I had had contact during various periods of my 79 years now got in touch with me again, including people for whose salvation I had prayed decades before.

Some had become Christians earlier. Some Corrie led to the Lord as a result of the program. She encouraged her friends:

God works sometimes slowly, but His work is perfect. Have you already prayed a long time for your son, husband, wife or neighbor? The devil will tell you, "You see, God does not hear you. How long have you already prayed now?" He is a liar. Do not listen to him. Not one prayer is lost. The devil often laughs when we are up to our eyes in work. He giggles when we make plans, but he trembles when we pray.

The Hiding Place

At the start of their work together neither Corrie nor Ellen could have imagined the extraordinary results of the publication of the book *The Hiding Place* in 1971 and the release of the movie of the same name four years later. It all began with prayer.

As we have seen, Corrie had prayed for many years that *A Prisoner and Yet . . .* would be made into a movie. But God had a different plan, and before there could be a movie a new book had to be prayed into being. While co-writers John and Elizabeth Sherrill were working with Brother Andrew on his book *God's Smuggler*, Andrew told them fascinating stories about his friend

Corrie's travels behind the iron curtain. At first they wondered if some of those stories could be part of Andrew's book, but finally they said, "We could never fit her into the book. She sounds like a book in herself." Shortly afterward the Sherrills met Tante Corrie when she gave her testimony at a church in Germany, and so it happened that plans were made for a new book about her.

In April 1969 Corrie wrote to her prayer partner friends:

Friends of mine in the U.S.A., John and Elizabeth Sherrill, are writing a book with me about my life. In January Mrs. Sherrill came to Holland as she wanted to see my hometown, Haarlem, and meet people here who could give information for the book. Together we visited many places, among them the prison in Scheveningen, where I was three months in solitary confinement.

The prison chaplain helped us get permission to see the prison inside. He also invited me to speak to the prisoners. What a joyful opportunity! In that building, where once I had suffered so much I spoke to the men and stood, as it were, beside them.

Although the reason for my imprisonment was different from theirs—as I had done something good (saving Jewish people during the last war)—I did not feel myself better than the criminals. It is by the grace of God that I am not a criminal myself. My sins are what you may call "decent sins." And although I am not guilty in the eyes of a human judge, still in the eyes of God I have been just as guilty as one who has committed a murder. For hatred was once in my heart, and in the eyes of God that is the same as murder. I brought a message to the men about our riches in Jesus Christ, which we can enjoy in the most difficult circumstances.

In Haarlem we saw the police station where my whole family and about 35 of our friends were kept before we were brought into the prison. It was there that for the last time we were together as a family.

During Mrs. Sherrill's visit we met several people who played a part in my life in that time of war. One of them was Eusie, the Jewish man full of humor who hid in our house. This time,

25 years later, he told me, "I appreciated it so much that I was treated in your house as a real friend of the family, and not just a Jew who needed to have a hiding place." And that is exactly what we all thought of him—a real friend of the family, as we all liked him so much. He is now a cantor-rabbi.

At the end of her visit to Holland, Mrs. Sherrill said that both she and her husband are praying much for guidance in all that writing a book involves. Will you pray with us that this book may become one hundred percent a blessing in the Kingdom of God? Thank you.

Then in April 1971 she wrote:

Sometimes I could not understand why the book has not been finished. The Lord used Catherine Marshall to tell me what the difficulty was. The last chapters tell about the sufferings of Betsie and about her death in the concentration camp. It was very hard for Tibby Sherrill to write these last chapters because she is living what she describes. That is why this last part of the book is such a great strain for John and Tibby Sherrill. Thank you for your prayers for them. I believe that this book will be a great blessing for many people, and I am sure that the Lord will use it to reach many more than my other books have done. The name of the Lord will be glorified. Hallelujah! Keep praying!

Four months later Corrie announced the publication of her book, at last with a name, *The Hiding Place*. It was released in the autumn of 1971 and quickly became a bestseller.

Movie Production Begins

Corrie had met Billy and Ruth Graham for the first time in the 1960s. Ruth was one of the first people to see the potential for a film in *The Hiding Place* book.

World Wide Pictures, the filmmaking arm of the Billy Graham Evangelistic Association, was headquartered in the Los Angeles area at that time. In 1972 Corrie wrote to a friend:

Next week we go to Glendale to meet the people of World Wide Pictures. Billy Graham is very happy with the book and that it can be worked out in a movie. It surely will reach many more people than we have ever been able to reach. I am so thankful. John and Elizabeth Sherrill's book is a good seller and has opened many doors and hearts for me. In April I will be 80 years old, and it seems that the Lord gives me more and more joyful work to do. I feel so privileged.

God uses Ellen much. Her testimonies are so powerful and always bring a blessing. We both feel happy to be in the USA.

Corrie was involved in the making of the movie from the start, enlisting the help of her prayer partners in the early days of planning.

With *The Hiding Place* there is better material for a movie than with *A Prisoner and Yet* . . . . Billy Graham's World Wide Pictures will make it. But . . . a movie is not a book. God needs to do miracles in many ways: a scriptwriter, then finances, the right cast and many other things. I ask your special prayer for this.

Corrie's Eightieth Birthday

On April 15, 1972, Corrie celebrated her eightieth birthday, first with friends at Cape Cod. She described the event:

I wore the long dress my friends in Scottsdale gave me. It was very *gezellig:* There were many bouquets and even real Dutch tulips and more than sixty smiling faces. Then there was a three-tiered cake with eighty candles on it! I am afraid it took me three puffs to blow them all out. Finally we stood and sang *Stand up, Stand up for Jesus,* and the thing I want most for this

Corrie, U.S.A., 1974   PHOTO COURTESY OF THE CORRIE TEN BOOM HOUSE FOUNDATION

coming year is to "stand" for Jesus. He has stood with me for 80 years, so I think I can trust Him for the rest.

Some weeks later, Corrie again celebrated her eightieth birthday when she returned to Holland. Among her guests was Loren Cunningham, leader of Youth With A Mission, whose work she prayed for and encouraged. She called him at his mission base in Switzerland and asked if he would come to pray for her that the Lord would give her a new ministry. So Loren drove from Switzerland to Corrie's party and prayed just as she asked—for a new ministry—but he also prayed something for which Corrie had not asked—that God would extend her life and work by another ten years.

At the end of her sabbatical year in Uganda with Conny, Tante Corrie had asked the Lord to give her another ten years of fruitful work. At the time of her eightieth birthday in 1972, the Lord had already given her seven of those years, and their fruitfulness and effectiveness were increasing by the day.

Could there really be another ten years—not just of life but of real work? Tante Corrie was not happy when she was not working. Would she still be working when she was ninety? It is probable she did not ponder Loren's prayer for long. Her times were in God's hands. I am sure she thought that if she were to live until she was ninety, they would be good and blessed years, for God never makes a mistake.

A Surprising World Premiere

The world premiere of *The Hiding Place* movie was scheduled for the evening of September 29, 1975, in Beverly Hills. The stars of the movie, other prominent actors and actresses and friends—even some from Europe—were present. The audience had mainly filled the theater when a sound like a rifle shot rang out, after which everybody was requested to leave the theater, which was filling with tear gas. It was later learned that this was the work of a member of the American Nazi party, apparently as a gesture of hatred against love for the Jews shown in the movie.

Corrie wrote:

> The Lord allowed it—otherwise, it would never have happened. How easy it is to become unforgiving at such a very important moment. But it seemed the Lord was teaching us in a very practical way the very lesson the film will bring to people. "Love your enemies, and forgive."

Corrie and Pam, Shalom House, Placentia, California, 1977   PHOTO CREDIT: RUSS BUSBY

A most wonderful thing happened that night. Across the street from the theater World Wide Pictures had arranged for bleachers so that people could sit and watch the many movie stars and others who came to the premiere. The street was roped off and when everyone had to leave the theater, the street was available for them.

Pat Boone, who was the M.C., was ready to go on, thinking that after the firemen had aired out the whole place everyone could return, but after ten minutes the manager of the theater told us that the stench was too much and the premiere could not continue. But we had a marvelous time out in the street, a place where we never could have had a street meeting. Billy Graham spoke, and Bev Shea sang *How Great Thou Art.* Cliff Barrows and Pat Boone led the singing. Many Hebrew songs were sung. It was all so different from what had been planned. But one thing is sure—Jesus got all the glory.

And, of course, the publicity generated by the tear gas incident resulted in many more people viewing the film. It was to become World Wide Pictures' most successful film.

Ellen Marries

In October 1975, a month after the release of the movie, Corrie and Ellen traveled to Oral Roberts University in Tulsa, Oklahoma, to fulfill speaking appointments. It was to mark the beginning of a big change in both their lives, for Ellen was to meet Bob Stamps, who had been chaplain at ORU for eight years.

Some months later, Ellen wrote to prayer partners:

"Delight yourself in the LORD and He will give you the desires of your heart. Commit your way to the LORD; trust in Him, and He will do this" (Psalm 37:4, 5).

In October 1975 two worlds met, and two prayers began to be answered. Two people had been praying that the Lord would lead them to the person whom God had prepared. Then Tante Corrie prayed for us: "Lord, thank You for not taking my daughter away, but for giving me a son."

Ours has been an international romance. Since the evening that Tante Corrie prayed for us, Bob and I have met in many different places.

Ellen announced that her wedding would be on August 1, 1976, in Holland, with a reception in Bob's hometown of Jasper, Texas, and then a dedication service at Oral Roberts University as soon as the students returned from summer vacation. And she said, "I have to thank many people, most of all Tante Corrie for all her love and care all of these years."

"How faithfully Ellen helped me in the nearly nine years we spent together, working in many different countries," wrote Corrie to her friends. "How the Lord is going to use her together with Bob."

And so it came about that I became part of the plan God had for the end of Corrie's life. When Ellen passed the care of Corrie over to me in April 1976, we did not know that another kind of imprisonment would be waiting for the one who had become a legend in her own already long lifetime.

twelve

I Am Yours!

1976–1983

$\mathcal{I}$ became Tante Corrie's companion only six months after the release of *The Hiding Place* movie. At the end of the movie the real Corrie ten Boom speaks to the audience. It should have been no surprise to me, then, when our international travels together began in April 1976, that she was widely recognized by American Christians who had seen the movie. "Recognized" is too mild a word. Mobbed is perhaps more descriptive. For the extroverted Tante Corrie this was no ordeal. The more people the merrier, as far as she was concerned. She found one thing, though, a bit of a trial.

She had cautioned me before we left Holland, "Americans like to hug necks." Part of my job was to try to shield her from neck huggers, many of whom we encountered at airports. Her dislike of that particular display of affection, however, had nothing to do with her love for and acceptance of people. When countless people asked her to pray for them she would say, "Let's go to the Lord right now." It did not matter how public the place. First things were always first with Tante Corrie. There was so much to do and so little time in which to do it, she often told me.

She met and prayed with people everywhere, and during those first few months of our work together we encountered people from Toronto, Honolulu, New York, Massachusetts, Charlotte, Williamsburg, Knoxville, Tulsa, Dallas, Des Moines, Chicago, Miami, Los Angeles, San Diego and San Jose. Tante Corrie did not like small talk, being put on a pedestal or any kind of silliness. She was not pious, staid, old-fashioned or prudish. She simply could not waste time.

I like people, too, but my personality is introverted. I like space and room to think. Whereas constant contact with people energized Tante Corrie, it had the opposite effect on me. To receive energy I needed to be alone and quiet for at least part of the day. That was hard to acquire in 1976 and 1977, but the next year there would be quietness such as I could never have imagined.

Corrie's books and the movie spread widely, and she received countless invitations to speak. To conserve her strength it became necessary to hold meetings in large venues where the maximum amount of people could listen to her messages. They were always the same: "God's light is stronger than the deepest darkness. Forgive your enemies. Live as rich as you are in Jesus Christ. Are you a child of God? If not, come to Jesus. Jesus is victor. There is only one person who cannot come to Him, and that is the one who thinks he is too good to come."

At the beginning of 1977, because it was becoming harder for foreigners to renew U.S. visitors' visas for more than a short time and because by now most of her work was carried on in the United States, Tante Corrie and I applied for and received resident alien status from the American consul in The Hague. This meant that we both could return to America for an indefinite time. Corrie, however, never became a U.S. citizen. The reason was quite simple. "As a Girl Scout I pledged total loyalty to the Queen of the Netherlands, and I will never disown her," she explained to inquirers.

When she left Holland in January 1977 it was for the last time. The remaining six years of her life would be spent in the United States. I wonder if she knew it.

Shalom House

For some months, even before we had to leave America to obtain resident status, Corrie had talked increasingly about having a home in the United States. Her heart was showing signs of slowing down, and she was often tired. I never saw her give in to this, however. She worked very hard, but wanted to find a home in Southern California near her board of directors for "Christians Incorporated," the organization set up some years earlier to handle correspondence, speaking and business arrangements for her. She also wanted to be near World Wide Pictures, with whom she hoped to make several more movies suitable for showing in churches. "So that I do not have to travel much anymore," she explained.

She would have liked to live near the ocean but relinquished that idea as soon as she learned the high prices of coastal property. After a short search, she rented a house in Placentia, about halfway between the ocean, which we visited quite often, and the studios of World Wide Pictures.

On February 28, 1977, 33 years to the day from her arrest in 1944, Corrie moved into her house. She took me by the waist and swung me 'round. *"We hebben een huis! We hebben een huis!"* ("We have a house!") She had no furniture, but when churches in the neighborhood learned of the famous newcomer, several showers were arranged. In a short time her home was furnished.

"The whole atmosphere of the house is one of peace, so I have named it Shalom, the Hebrew word for peace," she told her visitors.

Tante Corrie was extremely happy with her home. It was fairly simple and rather dark inside but was certainly adequate for her needs. It had a bedroom for both of us, a bedroom for visitors and a bedroom that we turned into an office. And it had a garden, with flowers back and front. Somebody even gave her a small lemon tree. With great interest she checked it every day on her walk through her yard. First came buds, then flowers. Would it really bear lemons one day? She was grateful for everything—the birds, flowers, receiving friends, getting to know the neighbors. And what probably made her happiest of all was the fact that she no longer had to travel and could carry out her work in one place with her own desk and books around her.

Corrie's publisher saw her delight and invited her to write a booklet, *A Tramp Finds a Home*. Ever a planner, she wrote:

> The Lord Jesus has the first place in this house. He has given us much important work to do here, and it is because we are doing His will that He blesses the home. Apart from the writing of books and the making of films there is intercession from this house, plus counseling personally and by telephone and letter. Through reading books and magazines that inform us of current events, we keep ourselves up-to-date with local, national and international affairs. We are aware that we are living in a time of crisis in world history. I pray often, "Lord Jesus, come quickly and make all things new." But in the meantime we want to point people to the Lord Jesus Christ, through whom they can live victoriously.[1]

Life with Tante Corrie

It was important to Corrie, however, that we stop work in the evenings. She and I sat together often in the living room on a white semicircular sofa, talked about the day, embroidered—it would not have been my choice, but Tante Corrie never did nothing!—and read books together, sometimes reading to each other. While we were together we shared everything, even the same book. It was *gezellig*. And during the day Tante Corrie took opportunities to read Christian books as she had done in all the decades of her travels and in her youth.

It was not always easy to live with Corrie! Her determination, dogged hard work and stubbornness were often hard to handle. But I am sure it was sometimes equally difficult for Corrie to live with me. "You are as stubborn as a mule," friends have told me more than once.

But we loved each other dearly, and "walking in the light" was part of our daily practice. When tensions came between us, when we needed to forgive each other of anything, it happened before the sun went down.

An example of this had to do with the simple matter of a picture. She asked me to take care of the framing of a copy of a Rembrandt etching. Corrie loved having her own walls. "This is *my* home," she wrote to her friends. "If you come and visit me, you will see the reproductions I had on the walls in earlier days, my portraits and the paintings I like."

Visitors would indeed see her portraits and paintings. Few were valuable, and most were reproductions. She hung them everywhere. People peered down from fading photographs on the mantelpiece. Pictures she had been given graced the most unlikely walls sometimes. It did not matter to her whether frames matched or whether items were hung in a standard order. She knew exactly how she wanted things arranged.

But Tante Corrie did not know the cost of items like framing, and when I arrived back with the etching she was not at all happy with me for spending about $45 on a suitable frame. She was very frugal and let me know she considered it a wasteful purchase. Her displeasure did not last long, though.

A Tramp Finds a Home

One day she told me a story that helped me understand why she was so overjoyed with her rented house, which she made sure I understood was as much mine as hers. We were sitting together on the white sofa. The oil painting of her father—the one that the city of Haarlem presented to him on his eightieth birthday and that Corrie found when she returned home from Ravensbrück—hung behind us on the light beige wall, and a round lamp hanging from a chain shed a golden light from above us. It was peaceful in Shalom House. Each of us had our handwork. She told me the story of the parting of the ways between her and the staff of the Zonneduin rehabilitation center in the mid-'60s. The misunderstanding was caused partly by Corrie's absences from Holland on her long world journeys. Her vision for the house and that of the staff who ran it for her changed as the years progressed and two different ministries emerged. But it was a big blow to Corrie when Zonneduin's staff asked her to leave the house and the room in which she had some items of furniture and other belongings. She wrote in *A Tramp Finds a Home:*

> Once, years ago, I decided to stop the life of a tramp. In Zonneduin, a house in Holland that we had arranged for people who needed to rest, I had one room that I called mine.
>
> To demonstrate to myself that that room would be my home, I opened a drawer where I kept my little pictures and photographs and put them on the walls; here, there and everywhere, almost like a child who arranges his room.
>
> The Lord said no to my desire to stop the life of a tramp and I obeyed, going back to my travels. When I returned to the room after some time, I found that all my little pictures had disappeared, having been removed by people who thought it strange to cover walls with childish pictures. They were right . . . they were fellow workers, and they told me that I was no longer welcome in Zonneduin. I left, and I was wounded.

Corrie forgave her friends, though. She was able to pray:

> Thank You, Father, that Your love in me is victorious over my resentment.
>
> Soon I understood that it was God's will that I went on with my life as a tramp.

Now, in my own home, which was in the Lord's plan for me but at a later date, I put more and more pictures on the walls, and I know I am allowed to do it.[2]

Her Final Works

In the eighteen months between her moving into her home in February 1977 and the stroke that took her powers of communication on August 23, 1978, the former tramp for the Lord was enabled to carry out many of her plans, including the making of filmed messages—a message especially for prisoners called *One Way Door;* a film with American Indians on her 86th birthday; and a film that was in progress at the time of her stroke, later entitled *Jesus Is Victor: A Personal Portrait of Corrie ten Boom.*

Although she mainly "stayed put," as she liked to express it, among other engagements she spoke in San Quentin State Prison, traveled to Tulsa, Oklahoma, for the baptism of Ellen's son, Peter John (who would later be joined by a sister) and took part in Christian Booksellers' conventions in Kansas City and Denver. Six books were published.

Corrie ten Boom's final work was on behalf of prisoners. As well as making a movie for them and writing a book, *He Sets the Captives Free,* she wanted to start an organization that would act as an umbrella for all ministries to prisoners so that one organization could learn from and help another, pooling resources on a national level. In the days leading up to her stroke most of her time was spent on behalf of prisoners.

A Different Kind of Imprisonment

And then on August 23, 1978, life changed radically. Tante Corrie had the first of several strokes that would gradually weaken her through the years that remained.

189

Many have asked why the Lord allowed His gifted child to spend nearly five years unable to do the work she loved, unable to speak, unable to read, write or comprehend in the normal way. I do not know. Neither did she, I am sure.

In a way it was another kind of imprisonment, but a precious one. The Lord had locked Corrie up with Himself.

At first it was hoped that she would regain some of her faculties of comprehension, but as the weeks turned into months with little improvement, I often thought about a letter Corrie had sent to a lady named Roberta shortly before her stroke. Roberta had written with questions about the reasons for suffering, and I had typed out Corrie's reply:

> The answer to the question about why there is suffering in the world is because there is sin in the world. There will be no end to suffering until the Lord Jesus comes and makes everything new. I do not understand, just like you, why He allows Christians to suffer, but I know that even then God is the God of love. He makes all things work together for good to those who love Him. I did not understand why my nephew and father and sister died . . . but I see now that their lives and deaths were used to bless very many thousands of people all over the world.
>
> When we love God and are trusting the Lord Jesus, it can be compared to an embroidery. God is making the embroidery. He sees the top. You and I see the underside. One day we will see the top, too. It is beautiful, but now you and I can know that only by faith in the Lord Jesus.

Many stroke patients suffer brain damage and resulting behavioral changes, causing situations that are often very distressing to their families and friends. In many cases the patients are deeply committed Christians. Why the Lord allows this is part of the mystery of suffering. One day we will understand.

As for Corrie, during her very slow decline her personality was not different. Although she became extremely weak physically, she took as large a part in the household as her disabilities allowed, even though she was confined to bed for most of those five years of silence. We worked out a system of communication, we prayed together, and we laughed, too. Many helped me in providing care for her.

She Wanted to "Die in the Harness"

Corrie had always longed to be able to work until the day the Lord came for her. When Miss Henrietta Mears, with whom she had spent time during visits to the West Coast of the United States and whom Corrie greatly respected, died on March 20, 1963, Corrie was in California. She had called to make an appointment to see Miss Mears again, but Miss Mears died before their planned meeting took place. Corrie wrote:

> I am sure that there is much work for her "in higher service," but what a loss it is for the people here. God used her mightily.
> Henrietta Mears "died in the harness." What joy to be able to work until the last day of your life! She was of my generation—only a few years older than I am. I may still go on until I pass the torch on to others or until Jesus comes. I pray that God will use me to redeem my time and trust Jesus more.

You may recall that Corrie made the same comment about Abraham Vereide when he died: "No sickness, no suffering," she wrote. "He really died in the harness at 82 years old." Should the Lord Jesus not return beforehand, and she believed He would, Corrie very much wanted to "die in the harness," too.

In those very long years at Shalom House between 1978 and 1983, I often wondered if Tante Corrie's serious brain damage allowed her to ponder the mystery of why she had apparently not been able to work until the last day of her life. Although she could not tell me, I think she did not. For one thing, she was never the pondering type! And I knew from close observation of her life when she was well that if she was still able to think in sequence, Corrie would have surrendered that desire to the Lord and accepted the present moment.

But I believe she *did* work until the last day of her life—and very effectively. She finished the race. She kept the faith. One of the greatest works the Lord did through her in those years, I believe, was her consistent witness to the dark, unseen and evil demonic powers that tried hard to silence her words "Jesus is victor." It was the ultimate test of her character, and the enemy did not succeed.

Still a Victorious Life

In my book *The Five Silent Years of Corrie ten Boom*,[3] written shortly after her death, I describe some of the things I observed in that time when the world of the former "tramp for the Lord" did not extend beyond the four walls of the front bedroom of her Shalom House in California. And yet in another way the world was still wide. We spent hours viewing some of the thousands of slides she had taken on her world travels. And part of each day was spent rearranging the many photographs and pictures on the walls of her own bedroom.

But there was nothing pathetic about her.

Corrie never showed any self-pity. As she had written about her first companion, Conny, years before, it was as if she did not know how to play the role of a patient. She could not speak, so I do not know what she was thinking. All I can tell you is the effect her still victorious life had on me. During those years, which sometimes seemed endless, when no plan could be made by the one who loved planning, she said to me without words: "I served Him in my youth; I will serve Him in my old age. I served Him in strength; I will serve Him in weakness. I served Him in life; and I will serve Him in death."

At 11:00 p.m. on her 91st birthday, April 15, 1983, the Lord undid the harness and took Corrie home.

Tante Corrie's Secret

What made Corrie the woman she was? Why is her story so powerful—even now, more than two decades after her death? Many factors combine. I have written about a few of them in this book—her grounding in the Dutch Reformed Church, her openness to receiving and obeying the Holy Spirit, her willingness to walk in the light, her determination to forgive, her pressing on to know more and more of the riches that are in Christ, and especially her steadfast belief that all her times were in God's very safe hands.

Corrie loved telling stories. *The Hiding Place* is powerful because story itself—the telling of the past course of a person's life for a positive and sometimes life-changing end—is powerful. It cannot be said often or strongly enough that each of us who loves the Lord Jesus has his or her own story without which every other Christian is the poorer. If you and I can learn to tell our stories—not necessarily in writing but in talking about them, in daily living and in worship—we will affect our world in ways that only eternity will tell.

Corrie learned to tell her story, and we can, too. But it will take passion—Corrie's kind of wholehearted passion for the Lord.

What if you and I do not have enough of that passion? How can we obtain it?

In her 1945 letter of forgiveness to the man who betrayed her to the Nazis, Corrie said, "If you find it difficult to pray, ask God to give you His Spirit. He will give faith in your heart." That is the best advice for you and me, too. We can ask God to give us the passion for Himself that we need in these dark days in which He planned for us to live and to tell our own stories about His love. There will be a price to pay, but He will help us to pay it if we ask Him.

All of this contributed to who Corrie was and what made her story so powerful. And yet Corrie herself summed up her secret in one short sentence.

One afternoon while she was still well, she entertained a young neighbor in the back garden of Shalom House. Anna had read *The Hiding Place* and was shy at first, but she soon relaxed when Corrie walked around the backyard with her, pointing to the flowers and to the lemons forming on the small tree.

As they sat down to drink tea, Anna asked, "What is your secret, Corrie?"

The answer was simple, of course. "Well, Anna, you see, one day I just said to the Lord, 'I am Yours from the tip of my toes to the top of my head.'"

Unconditional abandonment to God. Not her own faith. That was Corrie's secret.

Appendix 1

The Influence of Isaac Da Costa

Taken from *Father ten Boom, God's Man,* pages 29, 31, 32, 33

*C*orrie's passionate words about him and his work, written in the 1970s, show us the strong effect Isaac Da Costa had on the Ten Boom family and their faith:

He was a brilliant lawyer and a famous poet. As a result of the Enlightenment and the French Revolution, Europe had put reason above the Bible. Consequently there was a general relaxing of godly standards in all levels of society. Immediately after his conversion, Da Costa wrote a book titled *Objections Against the Spirit of This Age.* The basic theme was taken from Scripture.

For we are not fighting against people made of flesh and blood, but against persons without bodies—the evil rulers of the unseen world, those mighty satanic beings and great evil princes of darkness who rule this world; and against huge numbers of wicked spirits in the spirit world (Ephesians 6:12, TLB).

Immediately a storm of protest and contempt broke loose upon the courageous young lawyer. He was mocked and scorned in the press. A small circle of Hollanders stood with Da Costa. Among these was the Ten Boom family, including Willem. For these Christians, the clarion call of Da Costa meant the beginning of a new revival movement that left its mark on the whole spiritual atmosphere of nineteenth-century Holland. For many, the Bible was restored to its place of authority as the Word of God.

In 1851 Da Costa attended the World Conference of the Evangelical Alliance in London. Two days were set aside there to discuss the work among Jews in the various countries represented. In the detailed report of this conference I found an address by Da Costa that clearly states the reasons why he founded a number of prayer groups for Israel in various cities of the Netherlands. Here are a few thoughts from his interesting speech:

Brethren, I see you are all rejoicing in the blessings of Christian fellowship. Even so, I have come here to ask for tears. Tears and prayers. Yes, I myself must shed tears in your midst. For there is one nation that has not been represented at this great international gathering. It is God's own beloved people of Israel. Let us remember that our Savior, the Lord Jesus Christ, who is now interceding for us at the Throne of God, was born a Jew in a Jewish family in the nation of Israel. It is true that Israel missed God's target and was, for a time, set aside and dispersed among the nations. But the day will come when they will fall at the feet of their Messiah in true repentance and live!

On this occasion of the Great Exhibition, the Christians of Great Britain have called the nations together on their territory. The time will come when the King of the Jews will call a holy gathering in Jerusalem. This is not human imagination, but God's own Word through the witness of another Jew, the apostle Paul. He expresses this expectation in Romans

11:15:"If their [Israel's] rejection means the reconciliation of the world, what will their acceptance mean but life from the dead?" (RSV).

We all agree that a strong bond ties us to Israel. As to the past, Christianity is a fruit, an offshoot from the old people of God. As to the present, is not Israel's existence among the nations, despite centuries of hostility and persecution, one of the strongest proofs against the world's unbelief? And as to the future, how clearly the fulfillment of God's promises is related to the future of the world and the coming Kingdom of Christ! Well then, brethren! For these reasons I dare come to you with an earnest plea. It is a custom in Israel at certain great feasts to keep an open seat for the prophet Elijah. I request that you reserve an open seat for Israel in our midst today.

You lions of England and Scotland, give full honor to the Lion from the tribe of Judah who has conquered! You morning-watcher of the French people, announce the dawn of the day of His coming! You harp of Ireland, lead us in the song of expectation and longing of God's Church: "Come, Lord Jesus! Amen, come to bless and gather all the peoples of the world, also the long-rejected Israel in their midst! Amen."

Da Costa's work influenced my grandfather Willem to become one of the founders of the Society for Israel. Father often told us, "Love for the Jews was spoon-fed to me from my very youngest years." As a result, deep respect and love for the Jews became a part of our home life. How important childhood impressions are. Over the years we often experienced the truth of God's promise to Abraham, "And I will bless them that bless thee. . . ."

During the second half of the nineteenth century, the Jewish people slowly awakened to the need to return to their homeland. What had seemed an absolute impossibility for nineteen centuries—the establishment of a Jewish state in Israel, the land of the patriarchs—now became the vision of an Austrian reporter, Theodor Herzl. Herzl was not motivated by religious reasons. He thought only of survival for the Jews, but the return of the Jews to

Zion was the beginning of the fulfillment of the Old Testament prophecies concerning Israel's restoration.

Is it presumptuous to think that the small prayer meeting in Haarlem was connected with these events? I believe that God delights to use His children in the fulfillment of His plans for the world. I am sure He loves to use small people to do great things. How honored I am to be part of His plan!

Appendix 2

On Women and Preaching

In 1960, at the age of 67, in her bimonthly publication *It's Harvest Time*, Corrie ten Boom answered some questions put to her on women and preaching:

Question: Have you ever dealt with the difficulty that some people do not like it when women speak in public?

No, because I do not go where I am not allowed to speak.

Question: But do you yourself not have the feeling that you are being disobedient? Paul says in 1 Timothy 2:11–12 and in 1 Corinthians 14:34–35 that women must be silent.

Yes, Paul does say that, but we must understand what these words mean and what they do not mean. We must give them their place, of course, in the present age. Peter gave us a sketch of the present age in the words of Joel: "I will pour out my Spirit on all people. Your sons and daughters will prophesy" (Joel 2:28). Now, what is prophecy? First Corinthians 14:3 says it is "strengthening, encouragement and comfort."

199

Question: But didn't Peter mean that these things happened at the first Pentecost? (See Acts 2:16–21.)

Yes, they partly happened then. "This that you are now witnessing," says Peter. But in carrying on with the quotation he proceeded to tell about things that were not then happening. "Blood, and fire, and vapor of smoke" have not yet come to pass, and neither has the sun yet been turned into darkness nor the "moon into blood." We know from other Scriptures (e.g., see Matthew 24:29, Revelation 6:12) that these things will happen before the return of the Lord. We live in days past the beginning of the prophecy and before the end of it.

In Acts 2:18 we read, "Even on my servants, both men and women, I will pour out my Spirit in those days, and they will prophesy." There is no distinction of race in this verse; the power is to any devoted servant of Christ, Jew or Gentile, male or female. The 120 on the first Pentecost included certain women, and they all were filled with the Spirit and spoke languages they had never learned (see Acts 2:4–11).

In 1 Corinthians 11:5, we find that women prophesied in the assembly, and this was not forbidden by Paul but merely regulated, the covering of the head being commanded. This verse also tells that women prayed in the Church. In Acts 21:9 we are told about Philip's four daughters who prophesied—not because the prophesying of women was rare, but that it was unusual for four women in one family to do so.

Question: But what about 1 Corinthians 14:34–35, where it is clearly said that women must keep silent in the churches?

I believe that this must be interpreted in the light of these other Scriptures and not in conflict with them. Here is meant silence whilst another is speaking. ("Let them ask their own husbands at home.") Miriam, Deborah, Anna, a prophetess—these are good company for me. And Psalm 68:11 in the original gives them and me the encouragement: "The women that publish good things are a great host." There is one thing that a man or woman cannot do without: the anointing of the Holy Spirit that equips us to speak for God (see Acts 2:18).

"Open your eyes and look at the fields! They are ripe for harvest" (John 4:35).

Appendix 3

Ten Boom Family Resources and Timeline of Corrie ten Boom's Life

I am indebted to researcher and author Emily S. Smith for the following timeline of the Ten Boom family and their family tree. These resources enable the reader to trace many of Tante Corrie's family relationships; to place various members of the family, including the dates of their births and deaths; and to follow the timing of events in Tante Corrie's life and travels in considerable detail.

My warmest thanks go to Emily and to Frits Nieuwstraten, director of the Corrie ten Boom House Foundation in Haarlem, the Netherlands, for granting permission for us to include these meticulous and impressive pieces of work.

This timeline and family tree appear in the book entitled *A Visit to the Hiding Place: The Life-Changing Experiences of Corrie ten Boom*, written by Emily S. Smith and published by the Corrie ten Boom House Foundation. They are reproduced here with permission. This permission covers use in all languages and all editions throughout the world.

For more information about the centuries-old house in Haarlem containing the hiding place, now a museum, visit www.Corrie tenBoom.com

The Ten Boom Family

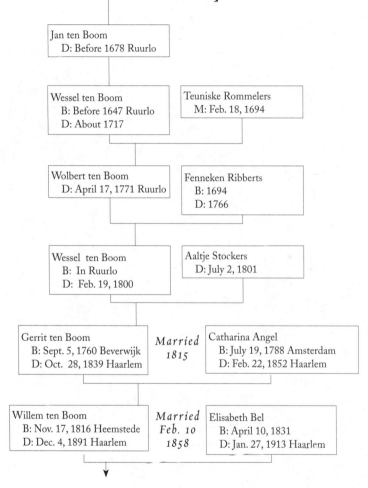

Jan ten Boom
D: Before 1678 Ruurlo

Wessel ten Boom
B: Before 1647 Ruurlo
D: About 1717

Teuniske Rommelers
M: Feb. 18, 1694

Wolbert ten Boom
D: April 17, 1771 Ruurlo

Fenneken Ribberts
B: 1694
D: 1766

Wessel ten Boom
B: In Ruurlo
D: Feb. 19, 1800

Aaltje Stockers
D: July 2, 1801

Gerrit ten Boom
B: Sept. 5, 1760 Beverwijk
D: Oct. 28, 1839 Haarlem

Married 1815

Catharina Angel
B: July 19, 1788 Amsterdam
D: Feb. 22, 1852 Haarlem

Willem ten Boom
B: Nov. 17, 1816 Heemstede
D: Dec. 4, 1891 Haarlem

Married Feb. 10 1858

Elisabeth Bel
B: April 10, 1831
D: Jan. 27, 1913 Haarlem

All locations in the Netherlands, unless noted.
Van Woerden information verified by Inge van Woerden. Other information provided by Hendrik ten Boom, Chief of Archives, Rotterdam (nephew of Casper).

203

Casper ten Boom (Papa) B: May 18, 1859 Haarlem D: March 9, 1944 Den Haag	Married Oct. 16 1884	Cornelia Johanna Arnolda Luitingh (Mama) B: May 18, 1858 Amsterdam D: Oct. 17, 1921 Haarlem

Elisabeth ten Boom (Betsie)
B: Aug. 19, 1885 Amsterdam
D: Dec. 16, 1944 Ravensbrück
C.C., Germany

Willem ten Boom
B: Nov. 21, 1886 Amsterdam
D: Dec. 13, 1946 Hilversum

Married
August 23 1916

Christina van Veen (Tine)
B: May 4, 1884 Utrecht
D: March 19, 1958
Hilversum

Casper ten Boom
B: July 13, 1917
D: About 1980

Hermiana Johanna ten
Boom (Hemmie)
B: Dec. 30, 1918 Made
D: Oct. 14, 1950 Hil-
versum

Christiaan Johannes ten
Boom (Kik)
B: May 27, 1920 Zuijlen
D: 1945 in or after
Bergen-Belsen C.C.,
Germany

Cornelia Arnolda Johanna
ten Boom (Nolly)
B: Dec. 16, 1921 Zuijlen
D: May 31, 1983 Maarn

Hendrik Jan ten Boom
B: Sept. 12, 1888
Amsterdam
D: March 6, 1889
Amsterdam

**Arnolda Johanna ten Boom
(Nollie)**
B: Sept. 25, 1890 Amsterdam
D: Oct. 22, 1953 Haarlem

*Married
July 23, 1919*

Frederik van Woerden
B: Dec. 20, 1890 Den Haag
D: Dec. 27, 1967 Bennebroek

**Cornelia Arnolda Johanna
ten Boom (Corrie)**
B: April 15, 1892 Amsterdam
D: April 15, 1983 Placentia,
CA, USA

Jacob Frederik van Woerden
B: May 14, 1920
D: 1982

Casper van Woerden (Bob)
B: May 18, 1921

Agatha van Woerden (Aty)
B: July 22, 1922

Pieter van Woerden (Peter)
B: Jan. 7, 1924
D: Sept. 6, 1990

Cornelia Arnolda Johanna
van Woerden (Cocky)
B: Sept. 24, 1926
D: July 28, 1997

Elizabeth Johanna
van Woerden (Els)
B: May 28, 1931

Ten Boom Family Timeline

This timeline contains many highlights in the Ten Boom family's life and in Corrie's ministry.

1837

Willem ten Boom (Corrie's grandfather) rents shop space and opens Ten Boom Horlogerie (watch shop) at Barteljorisstraat 19, Haarlem. In 1849, he is able to purchase the house for 1,200 guilders (FtB 27).

1841

Willem marries Geertruida van Gogh. They have thirteen children, but eight die before age four.

1844

Willem begins a prayer group to "pray for the peace of Jerusalem" (FH 15).

1856

Geertruida dies of tuberculosis at age 42 (FtB 26).

1858

Willem marries Elisabeth Bel February 10. They have six children; two die very young.

1859

Casper ten Boom (Corrie's father, the oldest of Elisabeth's children) is born May 18.

1884

Casper and Cornelia (Cor) Luitingh wed October 16. They reside at 28 Korte Prinsengracht, Amsterdam.

1885

Elisabeth (Betsie) is born August 19. Tante (Aunt) Anna (Cor's sister) comes to live with the family.

1886

Willem is born November 21.

1888

Hendrik Jan is born September 12 but dies March 6, 1889.

1890

Arnolda Johanna (Nollie) is born September 25. Ten Booms move to another house in Amsterdam (FtB 47).

1891

Grandfather Willem dies December 4, age 75.

1892

Cornelia Arnolda Johanna (Corrie) is born April 15 on Good Friday, about one month premature. Casper and family move from Amsterdam to a rented house in Haarlem so he can work in Ten Boom Horlogerie (FtB 52-53). Corrie is christened in the Dutch Reformed Church in July (PerL).

(From this point on, Corrie's age appears in brackets after the year. Corrie's birthday is April 15. The age listed for each year is her age following her birthday.)

1895 [3]

Tante Jans (Cor's sister) comes to live with the Ten Booms.

1897 [5]

Elisabeth (Casper's mother) moves from Barteljorisstraat 19, and Casper and family move in. Casper has house remodeled (FtB 55). Corrie prays and gives her life to Jesus (FH 24).

1909 [17]

Papa and Mama celebrate their 25th wedding anniversary. Corrie has completed primary and secondary school and studies at Domestic Science School (FtB 94). Ten Booms begin a missions study group in their home.

1910 [18]

Corrie takes classes at a Bible school in Haarlem for two years. She fails her final exam but receives her diploma eight years later (FH 93–94).

1911 [19]

Corrie works as an au pair (governess). Tante Bep (Cor's sister, who also lived with the Ten Booms) dies of tuberculosis at age 70. Corrie returns home (FH 75). Mama has slight stroke (FH 93).

1914 [22]

World War I begins. Corrie has appendectomy following months of bed rest (PerL).

1916 [24]

Willem is ordained. He is called to a church in Made; the family attends his first sermon. In Made, Corrie's friend Karel (not his real name) talks with her about their future together. They see each other again when Willem marries Tine van Veen August 23. In November, Corrie's heart is broken when Karel introduces her to his fiancée (HP 44–46). Willem pastors in Made four years, then in Zuijlen until 1926.

1918 [26]

Mama has major stroke (HP 48). As World War I ends, Ten Booms take in Willy, Katy and Mrs. Treckmann and her children Ruth and Martha, all from Germany (FH 102–4).

1919 [27]

Tante Jans dies from diabetes at age 71. Nollie marries Frederik "Flip" van Woerden July 23.

1920 [28]

Corrie completes her watchmaking apprenticeship in two factories in Switzerland (PerL).

1921 [29]

Mama dies October 17 at age 63. Corrie works in clock shop full-time; Betsie takes over housekeeping (FH 113).

1924 [32]

Corrie becomes Holland's first licensed woman watchmaker (HP 54).

1925 [33]

Tante Anna dies March 7 at age 64. Ten Booms begin to take in missionary children, three of them from one family: Puck, Hans, Hardy (FH 133), Lessie (FH134), Miep (FH 137) and Marijke (FH 140). In 1925, there are seven foster children total, known as the Red Cap Club. Corrie starts Christian girls' clubs; she works with them until 1940, when the Nazis order no group meetings (FH 125–82).

1926 [34]

Willem starts working with the Society for Israel. He goes to Leipzig, Germany, for one year to study for his doctorate, writes his thesis on racial anti-Semitism, and receives his Doctorate of Philosophy in 1928 (FtB 106).

1937 [45]

The 100th anniversary party of Ten Boom Horlogerie (watch shop) is held.

1940 [48]

Nazis invade Holland beginning May 10. Occupation lasts five years.

1941 [49]

In November, Corrie obtains help from Willem and Kik ten Boom to find a safe house for two Jewish friends (HP 69).

1942 [50]

Early spring, Corrie decides she must help save Jewish people. She becomes involved in the underground. Her nephew Peter van Woerden spends time in prison for showing patriotism to Holland (HP 73–75).

1943 [51]

Many Jews pass through the Ten Booms' home; most are relocated quickly. The names mentioned below are those who spent extended time with the family.

May 13
Ten Booms take young Dutchman Hans Poley into hiding; he becomes involved in the underground (RHP 15).

May 14
Hansje "Thea" Frankfort-Israels (Jew) moves in (RHP 29).

June
Mary van Itallie (Jew), Henk Wessels and Leendert Kip (underground workers) move in.

June 2
First drill for newly constructed hiding place is held (RHP 44).

June 28
Meyer Mossel, "Eusie," (Jew) moves in (RHP 47).

July
Henk Wiedijk (underground worker) moves in (RHP 64). Henk Wessels and Leendert Kip find other places to live, so Mr. de Vries (Jew) moves in (RHP 75).

August 14
Nollie is arrested for hiding a Jew. She spends four weeks in prison. Due to danger of Gestapo searching family members' homes, all in hiding leave Beje (Ten Booms' home) for other safe houses. Mary, Eusie, Henk and Hans return in three weeks. The others remain elsewhere (RHP 81–85). Mirjam de Jong (Jew) moves in (RHP 86).

September 30
All in hiding leave Beje again due to Gestapo worries (RHP 90). Mary, Eusie and Hans return in two weeks (RHP 96). Nel (Jew) and Ronnie Gazan (Jew) move in (RHP 97).

1944 [52]
January
Meta (Martha) and Paula Monsanto (Jews) move in (RHP 118). Paula leaves and moves in with Hans Poley's parents (RHP 120). Willem ten Boom's home is raided by Gestapo; no evidence is found (RHP 121).

February 5
Hans Poley is arrested trying to warn another family of a Gestapo raid (RHP 125). Because of danger, all in hiding leave Beje (RHP 139). Eusie, Mary, Martha and Ronnie return in one week (RHP 140). These are the four Jews living in Beje on February 28.

February 28
Gestapo agents raid Beje at about 5 p.m. (RHP 142). Six people illegally in the house (four Jews and two underground workers) run into the hiding place. About 11 p.m., Casper, Corrie, Betsie and Willem ten Boom and Nollie and Peter van Woerden are taken to the Haarlem jail along with about thirty others (PY 14, RHP 146). Six people remain in the hiding place while Nazis guard the house. Herman Sluring (Pickwick), Corrie's contact in the Dutch National Underground, is arrested elsewhere in Haarlem (HP 122).

February 29
The six family members are transferred to Scheveningen prison near Den Haag (PY 19).

March 1
After over 47 hours, all six in the hiding place are rescued at about 4:30 p.m. Eusie, Mary, Martha and Ronnie (Jews) are taken to new safe houses. Reynout Siertsema and Hans van Messel (underground workers) leave the Beje safely (RHP 160).

March 9
Casper ten Boom dies at age 84 (PY 22).

March 16
Corrie begins solitary confinement in cell 384 (PL 18).

April 15
Corrie spends her birthday in solitary confinement (HP 140).

June 5
Corrie and Betsie find each other as they are transported by train from Scheveningen prison to Vught Concentration Camp in Holland, arriving June 6 (PL 11).

September 4
Corrie and Betsie begin nightmare train ride—three days and three nights jammed into a boxcar. Their destination is Ravensbrück Concentration Camp near Berlin, Germany (PY 85).

September 8
Corrie and Betsie are officially registered as prisoners in Ravensbrück (PY 88).

December 16
Betsie dies in Ravensbrück at age 59 (LST 63).

December 25
After learning she is to be released, Corrie is put in Ravensbrück hospital due to edema (HP 202).

December 30
(or December 28—both dates appear on discharge) Corrie is released from Ravensbrück Concentration Camp (PY 88).

1945 [53]
January 1
As a free person, Corrie arrives in Berlin and finds a train to Groningen, Holland, where she spends ten days in a nursing home. One of her nurses, Truus Benes, is a friend from the YWCA (LST 69). Then Corrie recuperates with Willem and Tine for two weeks before returning to Haarlem (HP 205–8).

May 5
Liberation Day in Holland. Shortly afterwards, Corrie rents and opens part of Schapenduinen (the home of Mrs. Bierens-de Haan) as a Christian rehabilitation center for war victims (HP 212).

May 8
VE Day (Victory in Europe)

June 19
Corrie writes to Jan Vogel, the man who betrayed her family to the Gestapo, and forgives him (PL 81).

June
Corrie's first book, *Gevangene en Toch . . . (A Prisoner and Yet . . .)*, is published in Holland.

1946 [54]
Early in the year, Corrie travels by freighter to the United States (U.S.A.) to share her story. She begins in New York City and receives advice from Irving Harris. Then in Washington, D.C., she is helped by Rev. Abraham Vereide and his daughter Alicia, Marian Johnson, Mrs. Frank McSherry and Kate Cheney. From there, Corrie travels to speaking engagements across the country (HL 149–52). She writes a July prayer letter from Kansas having already worked in New York, Washington, D.C., Pennsylvania, Vermont, Michigan, Illinois and Canada. (Corrie's "work" is evangelism and discipleship.) In Canada, she is helped by Mrs. Bobbie Halliday. She works in California, Utah and Iowa. On December 13, Corrie's brother, Willem, dies at age 60 from tuberculosis of the spine, contracted in prison (HP 218). She returns to Holland after ten months abroad (PrL 6–47).

1947 [55]
Corrie continues work at Schapenduinen (PrL 6–47). She also works in Germany, where she meets a guard from Ravensbrück and forgives him (TfL 82). In September, she works in Canada (CP).

1948 [56]
On her birthday, Corrie speaks in Los Angeles at the University of California (*Contemporary Christian Acts* magazine 4–78). She attends a Youth for Christ conference in Switzerland (HL163).

1949 [57]
Corrie speaks in Germany and works in refugee camps there. With help from the German Lutheran Church, she rents and opens Darmstadt (a former concentration camp) for refugees. The Evangelical Sisterhood of Mary serves the refugees on an ongoing basis until the camp closes in 1960 (CP, HP 218). She also works in Switzerland and the U.S.A. (CP).

1950 [58]
Corrie works in California (HL163–64), Washington, D.C., (CP),

Michigan, Canada and Bermuda. In Bermuda, she speaks twenty times in one week (PerL 3–50). She returns to Holland by freighter and works several months in Germany (CP).

1951 [59]

Corrie works in Germany, England, Canada and the U.S.A. (CP). During this year, she returns to Holland to complete the purchase of the house Zonneduin for the Christian retreat and training center. It moves from its rented house, Schapenduinen (HL 166). She is associated with this work until 1966 (PerL).

1952 [60]

Corrie works in the U.S.A., and then, on her way to Japan, she stops in Hawaii and speaks sixteen times in four days (PerL 4–52). She works in Japan for nine months, partly with missionaries Father and Mother Mitchell (PerL).

1953 [61]

Corrie's second book, *Amazing Love,* is published. It is her first book printed in English. She works in Taiwan and visits leprosy patients with Lillian Dixon (PrL 1–53). She also works in the Philippines, New Zealand, Australia, Israel (CP), South Africa (Reim. 66), Spain and Switzerland (PrL 12–53). On October 22, her sister Nollie dies at age 63. Corrie is greatly affected by her sister's passing (TfL 62). In December, she is in Haarlem where she falls and injures her hip. She is cared for at Zonneduin (PrL 5-54).

1954 [62]

In early January, Corrie is prayed for; she receives the baptism of the Holy Spirit (TfL 62). She works five months in Germany (PrL 5–54). She meets a nurse who was cruel to Betsie in Ravensbrück and leads her to the Lord (HL 160). Corrie also works in the U.S.A. (PrL 10–54), Bermuda and Cuba (PrL 2–54). Her first book, *Gevangene en Toch* . . . , is translated and published in English as *A Prisoner and Yet* . . .

1955 [63]

Corrie works in Canada, Mexico and the U.S.A. (PrL 1–55, 5–55). This trip lasts sixteen months (PrL 1–56).

1956 [64]

Corrie works in Hawaii for one month, where she speaks at 85 meetings (PrL 5–56). Remainder of year she works in New Zealand and Australia with the Revival Fellowship Team of J. Edwin Orr (PrL 1956).

1957 [65]

Corrie continues her work with the Revival Fellowship Team in New Zealand and Australia for this entire year (PrL 1957). Her books *Not Good If Detached* and *Common Sense Not Needed* are published.

1958 [66]

Corrie works in India, Borneo, Korea, Japan and Formosa (IHT 1958). Having been christened as a child, she is baptized by immersion at the William Carey Baptist Church in Calcutta, India, on March 20 (PerL). The name of her personal updates changes from *Prayer Letter* to *It's Harvest Time*.

1959 [67]

Corrie begins the year working in Hong Kong, then in Vietnam and Europe (IHT 1959). She returns to Ravensbrück Concentration Camp to discover her release was a clerical error (HP 219).

1960 [68]

Corrie works in Germany, Spain, England, Switzerland and for three months in Israel (IHT 1960). In Switzerland, she meets Billy and Ruth Graham (LST 106). She begins traveling with a personal companion, Conny van Hoogstraten. They work together seven years (HL 176).

1961 [69]

Corrie works in India for three months, then in Africa for eight months (IHT 1961).

1962 [70]

Corrie works in South America and the U.S.A. (IHT 1962). On April 17, the Netherlands' Queen Juliana makes Corrie a Knight in the Order Oranje-Nassau (LST 102).

1963 [71]

Corrie writes about recent work in Bermuda and Canada (IHT 1–63). She works in the U.S.A. (IHT 3–63). She stays in Buenos Aires, Argentina, in the apartment of Dr. Gwen Shepherd for six weeks. This is the first time in sixteen years she has stayed in the same home that long. She speaks in many meetings and visits patients at Dr. Shepherd's hospital. Then Corrie works in Cordoba, Argentina (IHT 6–63, TfL 102) and Brazil (PerL 7–1963). She returns to Holland for hospitalization due to an infection of the liver (IHT 10–63). She flies to the U.S.A. December 31 (CP).

1964 [72]

Corrie works in the U.S.A. (CP), Germany, Poland and Finland (IHT 1964). Then she is diagnosed with hepatitis. Under doctor's orders, she takes a year off from working. Her sabbatical year begins in September. She spends the first two months receiving medical treatment in Bavaria, Germany; then she stays with her nephew Peter van Woerden and family in Switzerland (IHT 1964–65).

1965 [73]

The remaining months of her sabbatical year are spent with Harry and Evelyn Campbell in Uganda, East Africa (HL 177). During her "year off," Corrie occasionally speaks in prisons and churches in Kenya and Uganda (CP, HL 178). In October, she starts to work again in Tanzania, Kenya, Rwanda, Burundi, Congo and Uganda (CP, IHT 12–65/3–66).

1966 [74]

By the end of January, Corrie finishes four months of work in Africa by speaking in Congo, Kenya and Ethiopia (CP). Then she works in Canada and the U.S.A. (CP). For several months, she works in Russia and Eastern Europe (Hungary, Poland, Czechoslovakia), then Germany and Holland (CP).

1967 [75]

Corrie works in France and Indonesia (CP). She celebrates her 75th birthday in Vietnam. It is wartime, and she is working with missionary Brother Andrew (LST 89). When she returns to Holland, Baroness Elisabeth van Heemstra loans her an apartment to use as a "home base" whenever she is in Holland (HL 186). In the summer, Conny leaves to marry Lykle Hoogerzeil, a Dutch missionary doctor to India (ML 23, 28). Ellen de Kroon becomes Corrie's next personal companion. They work together for nine years. A car Corrie is riding in is involved in a serious accident, and her arm and shoulder are broken. She spends nine weeks in the hospital (HL 186). *Plenty for Everyone* is published.

1968 [76]
On February 28, Corrie is honored by Israel at Yad Vashem (Holocaust Memorial). She is asked to plant a tree in the Garden of the Righteous because of the many Jewish lives she and her family saved during World War II. She works in Israel, Holland, Germany (IHT 5–68), the U.S.A., England and Moscow (CP).

1969 [77]
Corrie begins the year in Switzerland, then works in France (IHT 4–69), the U.S.A. (CP), Moscow (CP), Kazakhstan, Tajikistan, Uzbekistan, Germany (IHT 1–70) and Cuba (CP). Corrie's book *Marching Orders for the End Battle* is published.

1970 [78]
Corrie works in Israel and Cyprus (IHT 5–70). Her former personal companion, Conny, dies of cancer. Corrie speaks at the funeral (HL 179). She returns to Holland for five months' rest—under doctor's orders (IHT 9–70), then works in Alaska and the northern U.S.A. (IHT 12–70). *Defeated Enemies* is published.

1971 [79]
Corrie spends five months in the U.S.A. (IHT 4–71), then works in Holland, the U.S.A. (IHT 8–70) and Canada (CP). *The Hiding Place*, by Corrie with John and Elizabeth Sherrill, is published in November (IHT 8–71).

1972 [80]
Corrie continues to work in the U.S.A. and Canada (IHT 1972).

1973 [81]
Corrie works in the U.S.A. (IHT 2–73). She begins calling her

personal updates *The Hiding Place Magazine,* which is regularly published into 1983. She works in the Netherlands Antilles (HPM Sm 73). In June, she speaks at the Billy Graham Crusade in Atlanta, Georgia (BGCA).

1974 [82]

The Hiding Place movie is filmed from March through June in Haarlem and England. Corrie visits the set (LST 110, HL 202). Corrie works in the U.S.A. and Israel (HPM Sm 74). In July, she speaks at Congress for World Evangelization in Switzerland (MY 122). *Tramp for the Lord,* by Corrie with Jamie Buckingham, is published. In November, she is interviewed at the Billy Graham Crusade in Norfolk, Virginia (BGCA).

1975 [83]

Corrie works in the U.S.A. for several months (HPM Sp 75) and in Bermuda (HPM W 75). The Beje opens as a museum, "The Hiding Place" (LST 98). On September 29, *The Hiding Place* movie is to premiere in Beverly Hills, California. Just as it is to begin, a suspected neo-Nazi group throws a tear gas bomb into the theater. Instead of viewing the movie, hundreds of people enjoy a street meeting with Corrie, Billy Graham, Pat Boone as the master of ceremonies, Bev Shea singing "How Great Thou Art" and Pat and Cliff Barrows leading singing. Newspapers and television carry the story internationally (LST 112). *The Hiding Place* is shown in movie theaters in many countries. In November, a member of the Evangelical Sisterhood of Mary comes to the Beje and presents Corrie with plaques that are hung in the hiding place (LST 98). *Prison Letters* is published.

1976 [84]

In January, Corrie is in Oklahoma (BGCA). In April, Pam Rosewell becomes Corrie's personal companion when Ellen de Kroon leaves to marry Bob Stamps, chaplain of Oral Roberts University (TH 16). Pam works with Corrie seven years. Their first trip is seven months long, working in Switzerland; Toronto, Canada; and the U.S.A. (Honolulu, Hawaii; New York; Wenham, Massachusetts; Charlotte, North Carolina; Williamsburg, Virginia; Knoxville, Tennessee; Tulsa, Oklahoma; Dallas and Waco, Texas; Des Moines,

Iowa; Chicago, Illinois; Miami, Florida; Los Angeles, Anaheim, San Diego, and San Jose, California) (SY 40, 42). On April 23, Corrie receives an honorary degree (Doctorate of Humane Letters) from Gordon College in Massachusetts (HPM Sm 76); then she spends three months in Holland (SY 49). *In My Father's House*, by Corrie with C. C. Carlson, and *Corrie's Christmas Memories* are published. The film *Behind the Scenes of The Hiding Place* is released.

1977 [85]

In January, "The Hiding Place" is closed as a museum because of too many visitors (HPM Sp 77). Corrie is the guest speaker at a Billy Graham Crusade in Gothenburg, Sweden, and then works in Switzerland (HPM Sp 77). Also in January, Corrie and Pam receive resident alien status in the U.S.A. and leave for Florida, where Corrie spends several weeks writing a book (HL 209, SY 50). Then she and Pam go to California to look for a house to rent (SY 49). On February 28, they move into "Shalom" house in Placentia, California (LST 120). Corrie works in New York and Florida (HPM Sm 77). On July 4, in Arizona, she is honored by CHIEF (Christian Hope Indian Eskimo Fellowship), receives a headdress and is welcomed into their tribes. In July, she attends a booksellers' convention in Kansas City and Denver and then goes to Oklahoma for the baptism of Ellen's son, Peter John Stamps. She completes a film made especially for prisoners, *One Way Door* (HPM F 77). On September 25, she speaks at San Quentin Prison, near San Francisco, California (LST 125). In October, Corrie is hospitalized to receive a pacemaker (SY 73). In November, she speaks in Portland, Oregon (HPM Jan 78). *Each New Day; Prayers and Promises for Every Day; He Cares, He Comforts;* and *He Sets the Captives Free* are published.

1978 [86]

On April 15, Corrie spends her birthday in Arizona making a film for American Indians (SY 82). She spends May and June working on the book *This Day Is the Lord's*, which is published in 1979 (ST 156). In the early summer, she works on the film *Jesus Is Victor* (SY 89). In July, she is honored with an evening called "Corrie: The Lives She Touched" (SY 91). On August 23, she suffers her first major stroke

(SY 102) and loses most of her ability to communicate (ST 163). Her books *Father ten Boom, God's Man*; *A Tramp Finds a Home*; and *Don't Wrestle, Just Nestle* are published.

1979 [87]

On April 15, Corrie celebrates her 86th birthday with a small party in the back garden (HPM May 79). In May, she suffers a second serious stroke, losing the use of her right arm and leg (SY 144, ST 169).

1980 [88]

In October, Corrie suffers her third serious stroke and is bedridden (SY 186).

1982 [90]

Corrie's book *Clippings from My Notebook* is published. It is a collection of notes she wrote and photographs she took during her many decades of travel. Corrie's evangelistic film *Jesus Is Victor* is released.

1983 [91]

On her 91st birthday, April 15, Corrie goes to heaven. She dies at approximately 11 p.m. (SY186). Her memorial service is held on April 22, with burial at Fairhaven Memorial Park, Santa Ana, California. Her evangelistic films *One Way Door* and *Corrie: The Lives She's Touched* are released. Her book *Not I, but Christ* is published this year in Dutch, in 1984 in English.

1985

Jesus Is Victor is published. It is a compilation of three of Corrie's books.

1988

On April 15, the Corrie ten Boom House opens as a museum in Haarlem, Holland.

1999

Reflections of God's Glory is published. It contains messages given by Corrie on Trans World Radio.

2002

Messages of God's Abundance is published. This contains additional messages given by Corrie on Trans World Radio.

2003

The Hiding Place movie on DVD is released by World Wide Pictures. It includes four of Corrie's other films: *Behind the Scenes of The Hiding Place, Jesus Is Victor, One Way Door* and *Corrie: The Lives She's Touched.*

Additional tributes given to the Ten Boom family: There is a Corrie ten Boomstraat (street) and a Casper ten Boomstraat in Haarlem, a Ten Boomstraat in Hilversum named for Christiaan ten Boom (Kik), and a Ten Boom School in Maarssen named for Corrie's brother, Willem.

Timeline References

BGCA   From the Corrie ten Boom Collection in the Billy Graham Center Archives, Wheaton College, Wheaton, Illinois.

CP   Corrie's passports, BGCA.

FH   *In My Father's House* by Corrie ten Boom with Carole C. Carlson. Grand Rapids, Michigan: Fleming H. Revell, a division of Baker Book House Company, 1976, 2000. 1976 edition co-published with Christian Literature Crusade, Fort Washington, Pennsylvania. All publications rights held by Baker Book House Company, Grand Rapids, Michigan.

FtB   *Father ten Boom: God's Man* by Corrie ten Boom. Grand Rapids, Michigan: Fleming H. Revell, a division of Baker Book House Company, 1978.

HL   *Corrie ten Boom: Her Life, Her Faith* by Carole C. Carlson. Grand Rapids, Michigan: Fleming H. Revell, a division of Baker Book House Company, 1983.

HP   *The Hiding Place* by Corrie ten Boom with John and Elizabeth Sherrill. Chappaqua, New York: Chosen Books LLC, 1971.

HPM   *Hiding Place Magazine*, a personal update from Corrie ten Boom, in the archives of the Corrie ten Boom House Foundation, Haarlem, Netherlands.

IHT   *It's Harvest Time*, a personal update from Corrie ten Boom, in the archives of the Corrie ten Boom House Foundation, Haarlem, Netherlands.

LST   *Corrie, The Lives She's Touched* by Joan Winmill Brown. Grand Rapids, Michigan: Fleming H. Revell, a division of Baker Book House Company, 1979.

MY   *My Years with Corrie* by Ellen de Kroon Stamps. Eastbourne: Kingsway Publications Ltd and Alresford: Christian Literature Crusade. Copyright: Fleming H. Revell, a division of Baker Book House Company, 1978.

NG   *Not Good If Detached* by Corrie ten Boom. London: Christian Literature Crusade, 1957. Publications rights held by Baker Book House Company, Grand Rapids, Michigan.

PerL   Personal letters from the Ten Boom family, in the archives of the Corrie ten Boom House Foundation, Haarlem, Netherlands.

PL   *Prison Letters* by Corrie ten Boom. Grand Rapids, Michigan: Fleming H. Revell, a division of Baker Book House Company, 1975.

PrL   *Prayer Letter*, a personal update from Corrie ten Boom. in the archives of the Corrie ten Boom House Foundation, Haarlem, Netherlands.

PY   *A Prisoner and Yet . . .* by Corrie ten Boom. London: Christian Literature Crusade, 1954. Publications rights held by Baker Book House Company, Grand Rapids, Michigan.

Reim.   *Het Leven van Corrie ten Boom* by Lotte Reimeringer-Baudert. Hoornaar, Netherlands: Gideon, 1985.

RHP   *Return to the Hiding Place* by Hans Poley. Elgin, Illinois: LifeJourney Books, an imprint of Chariot Family Publishing, a division of David C. Cook Publishing Company, 1993. Copyright: Hans Poley.

SY   *The Five Silent Years of Corrie ten Boom* by Pamela Rosewell. Grand Rapids, Michigan: Zondervan, 1986. Copyright: The Zondervan Corporation.

ST   *Safer Than a Known Way* by Pamela Rosewell Moore. Grand Rapids, Michigan: Chosen Books, Fleming H. Revell, a division of Baker Book House Company, 1988.

TH   *A Tramp Finds a Home* by Corrie ten Boom. Grand Rapids, Michigan: Fleming H. Revell, a division of Baker Book House Company, 1978.

TfL   *Tramp for the Lord* by Corrie ten Boom with Jamie Buckingham. Grand Rapids, Michigan: Fleming H. Revell, a division of Baker Book House Company, 1974, 2000. 1974 edition co-published with Christian Literature Crusade, Fort Washington, Pennsylvania. All publications rights held by Baker Book House Company, Grand Rapids, Michigan.

Dates for births, deaths, and marriages were obtained from official records.

Notes

Chapter 2: Corrie's Early Life and Influences

1. Corrie ten Boom, *In My Father's House* (Grand Rapids, Mich.: Revell, 1976), p. 17.
2. Ibid.
3. Hendrik Marsman (1899–1940), *Herinneringen aan Holland.* This is a free translation by the author. Publisher, if any, is unknown.
4. Ten Boom, *In My Father's House,* pp. 23–24.

Chapter 3: World War I

1. Corrie ten Boom with John and Elizabeth Sherrill, *The Hiding Place* (Washington Depot, Conn.: Chosen Books, 1971), p. 45.
2. Ibid., p. 47.
3. Ibid.

Chapter 4: The Years between the World Wars

1. Ten Boom, *In My Father's House,* paraphrased.

Chapter 5: "The Deepest Hell That Man Can Create"

1. H. R. Wilhemina, Princess of the Netherlands, *Lonely But Not Alone,* trans. John Peereboom (New York: McGraw-Hill, 1960), p. 147.
2. Ten Boom, *The Hiding Place,* p. 62.
3. Ibid.

4. Ibid., p. 64.

5. Hans Poley, *Return to the Hiding Place* (Elgin, Ill.: LifeJourney Books, an imprint of Chariot Family Publishing, a division of David C. Cook Publishing Company, 1993), p. 16.

6. Ten Boom, *The Hiding Place*, p. 192.

7. Ibid., p. 195.

8. Ibid., p. 196.

9. Ibid., p. 197.

10. Corrie ten Boom, *A Prisoner and Yet* . . . (Fort Washington, Pa.: Christian Literature Crusade, 1970), p.162. Similar words are used in *The Hiding Place*.

Chapter 6: Corrie Begins to Tell Her Story

1. Corrie ten Boom, *Tramp for the Lord* (Old Tappan, N.J.: Revell, 1974), p. 40.

Chapter 7: "We Are Able to Live as King's Children"

1. Ten Boom, *The Hiding Place*, p. 215.

2. Grant Colfax Tullar, original source unknown.

Chapter 8: In the Power of the Holy Spirit

1. Ten Boom, *Tramp for the Lord*, pp. 57–61.

2. Ibid., p. 61.

Chapter 10: When Bad Things Happen

1. Corrie ten Boom, *Not Good If Detached* (Grand Rapids, Mich.: Revell, 1966), pp. 40–42.

Chapter 12: I Am Yours!

1. Corrie ten Boom, *A Tramp Finds a Home* (Old Tappan, N.J.: Revell, 1978), p. 51.

2. Ibid., pp. 31–33.

3. Pam Rosewell, *The Five Silent Years of Corrie ten Boom* (Grand Rapids, Mich.: Zondervan Publishing House, 1986).

Index

Born near London, **Pam Rosewell Moore** has lived in the United States since 1976. That year she became companion to Corrie ten Boom, the Dutch Christian whose incarceration in a Nazi concentration camp during World War II is known to many through the book *The Hiding Place* and the film of the same name. It was Pam's privilege to live and work with Miss ten Boom from 1976 until her death in 1983.

After seeing the victorious end to Tante (Aunt) Corrie ten Boom's life, Pam wrote her first book, *The Five Silent Years of Corrie ten Boom* (Zondervan, 1986). This describes the last years of the Dutch evangelist's life, when she was crippled and silenced by successive strokes, and it also relates Pam's reactions to those events. *When a person cannot achieve in the normal way, where does his or her value lie?* This is the question the book asks of a society in which a person's worth often seems related to personal achievement.

In 1988 Pam wrote her second book, *Safer than a Known Way* (Chosen), which tells of her growing up in Hastings, Sussex, England, and coming to know the Lord Jesus Christ when she was 21. At that time she surrendered her own will to the will of God. Her previous reluctance to do so had lain in the fact that she thought he might want her to be a missionary—something she was sure she could never do. Missionaries were often required to do three things Pam knew were impossible for her—leave home and family, speak in public and lead a single life. But in the years following her prayer of relinquishment, she was to see the Lord fulfill her through the very things she had feared.

In 1966 Pam left England for a year of volunteer work as secretary to the Archbishop of East Africa in Nairobi, Kenya. In 1968 she joined the mission of Brother Andrew, God's smuggler, in the Netherlands. For more than seven years she saw God work miracles as teams transported Bibles and Christian books across the forbidding borders of Eastern Europe.

After her marriage to Carey Moore in 1986, Pam Rosewell Moore lived for two years in Waco, Texas, before the couple moved to Dallas in 1988. For the next fourteen years she worked at Dallas Baptist University, first as director of that institution's intercessory prayer ministry and then as director of spiritual life. Carey is Government Documents Librarian at Dallas Baptist University.

In 1991 Pam and Carey wrote their first book together. *If Two Shall Agree*, published by Chosen Books, addressed the need for Christian couples to pray together. This book was re-released in 1999 under the title *What Happens When Husbands and Wives Pray Together?* In 2000 a fourth book was published by the same company when Pam wrote *When Spring Comes Late: Finding Your Way through Depression*.

Pam, who speaks often at conferences and other meetings, and Carey Moore and their dogs, Annabelle and Toby, make their home in Waxahachie, Texas, just south of Dallas.